WHAT'S YOUR PERSONALITY TYPE?

Using the Dog Type Personality System for Business and Life Success

Gini Graham Scott, Ph.D.

Author of *Do You Look Like Your Dog?* **and** *Discover Your Dog Type*

USING THE DOG TYPE PERSONALITY SYSTEM FOR BUSINESS AND LIFE SUCCESS

Copyright © 2020 by Gini Graham Scott

All rights reserved. No part of this book may be used or reproduced by any means, graphic, electronic, or mechanical, including photocopying, recording, taping or by any information storage retrieval system without the written permission of the author except in the case of brief quotations embodied in critical articles and reviews.

TABLE OF CONTENTS

INTRODUCTION 5
PART I: HOW THE DOG TYPE SYSTEM WORKS 11
CHAPTER 1: RECOGNIZING THE FOUR DOG TYPES 13
    Are You a German Shepherd? 14
    Are You a Border Collie? 17
    Are You a Golden Retriever? 16
    Are You a Pomeranian? 15
CHAPTER 2: THE ROOTS OF THE DOG TYPE SYSTEM AND WHY IT WORKS 19
    The Myers-Briggs Type Indicator 20
    The DISC Personality Profile 23
    The Red-Blue-Yellow-Green Personality Type 29
    Some Modern Variations on the Red-Blue-Yellow-Green System 31
        Summing Up 35
CHAPTER 3: WHERE THE 4-DOG TYPE SYSTEM FITS 36
    How the Dog Type System Differs from Other Systems 36
    Why Choose the 4 Selected Dogs for the 4-Dog Type System 36
    The Key Characteristics of the Four Types of Dogs 37
PART II: APPLYING THE DOG TYPE SYSTEM 41
CHAPTER 4: UNDERSTANDING YOUR STRENGTHS AND WEAKNESSES 43
    When Strengths Can Help 43
    When Strengths Become Weaknesses 44
    What If You're a German Shepherd? 46
    What If You're a Pomeranian? 48
    What If You're a Golden Retriever? 50
    What If You're a Border Collie? 51
CHAPTER 5: ASSESSING HOW TO BETTER COMMUNICATE WITH AND INTERACT WITH OTHERS BASED ON THEIR DOG TYPE 54
    Adapting Your Approach to Others 56

    Relating to the German Shepherd (Red/Dominant Leadership Type) 57

    Relating to the Pomeranian (Yellow/Influencer/Fun Party Animal Type) 59

    Relating to the Golden Retriever (Green/Steady/Cool Supporter) 61

    Relating to the Border Collie (Blue/Conscientious/the Serious Fact Checker) ... 63

  Summing Up 64

CHAPTER 6: USING THE DOG TYPE SYSTEM IN DIFFERENT SITUATIONS 66

  Testing Out Whether the System Works for You 68

  Making a Sale of a Product or Service 70

  An Example of Adapting a Presentation to Make a Sale 71

  Looking for Clients or Referrals at a Networking Event 72

  An Example of Successfully Meeting a Prospect at a Networking Event 73

  Improving Your Relationships with Co-Workers, Your Boss, or Your Employees in the Workplace 75

    Examples of Using the Dog Type System in the Workplace 76

    An Example of Improving your Relationship in the Workplace. 80

  Getting a Job or Promotion 80

  Improving Your Relationships with Others in Your Personal Life 82

CHAPTER 7: QUICKLY IDENTIFYING THE DIFFERENT DOG TYPES 85

  Using the Dog Type Occupations, Thinking, and Emotional Orientations Chart 87

CHAPTER 8: PUTTING IT ALL TOGETHER 90

  Summing Up 90

  What's Next? 91

ABOUT THE AUTHOR 92

INTRODUCTION

The Dog Type system is a new approach to understanding yourself and others. You can use it to better communicate with others, improve your relationships in your personal life and at work, increase your business, and just have fun. It's based on knowing the types of dogs you and others like the most and least, and I wrote several previous books about it: *What's Your Dog Type?, Discovering Your Dog Type, Using the Dog Type System in Your Everyday life,* and *Using the Dog Type System for Success in Business and the Workplace.*

You can use this system both for personal growth and self-development and in business, to better deal with customers, clients, and co-workers and build a more effective team.

In this popular version of the system, you choose among four different types of dogs to guide the way you communicate and interact with others, based on the type of do you are each the most like.

The system has parallels with other popular systems for understanding yourself and dealing with others, except it uses dogs because they are so easily relatable, and this makes working with the system informative, insightful, and fun.

Some of these systems have become very popular in among persona and professional coaches and in the business world are these three systems:

- the Myers-Briggs system, which is a scale of four main categories – extraversion-introversion, feeler-thinking, perceiver-judger, and intuitive-sensor;

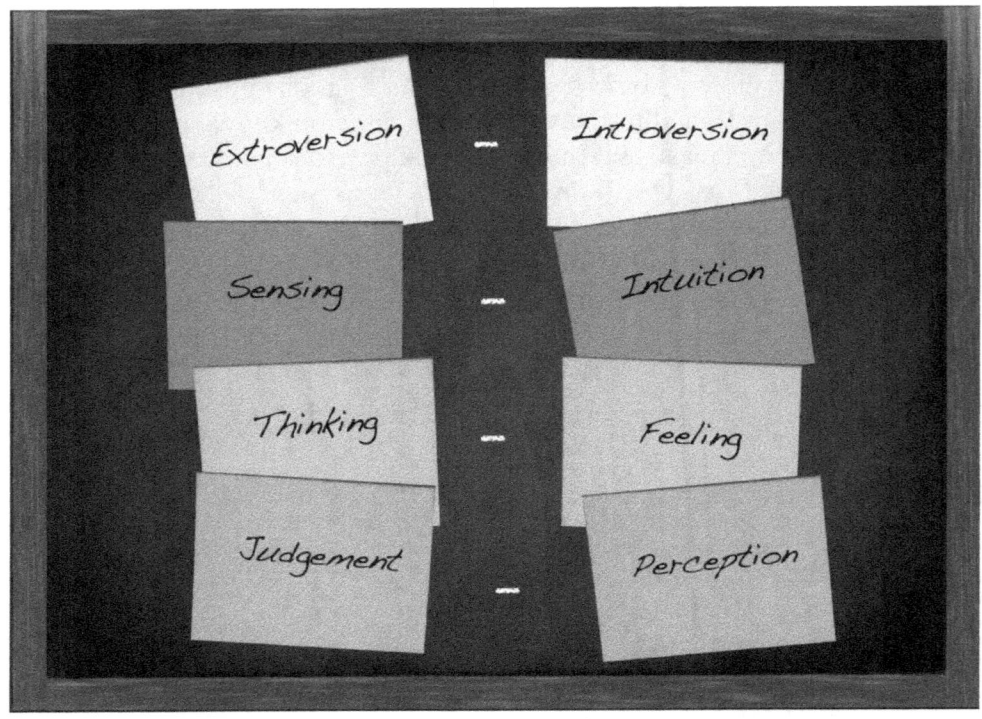

the DISC system, which is based on whether one's personality is characterized by dominance, influence, steadiness, or conscientiousness,

- the red, blue, yellow, and green personality type system. In this latter system, the reds are characterized as leaders, who are strong-willed, fast thinkers; the yellows, are sociable, friendly, party animals; the blues, are deep-thinking analytical types, and the greens are laid-back, friendly, and agreeable types; though in some color profiles, the yellow, blue, and green categories are switched.

Inspired by those systems, the Dog Type system has been developed, so you can quickly chose one of four types of dogs you feel best fits you or another person. Then, you can use that selection to best decide on how to communicate with and interact with, that person. For example, you can use knowing the person's personality type to better communicate in a personal relationship. You can better persuade someone to do something or make a sale. You can promote more cooperation and productivity in a work team. You can develop a presentation with different sections to appeal to each of the personality types.

Here's how it works. You choose the breed of dog you feel the most affinity for, the one you feel the next most connected to, and the one where you feel the least connection, and you do the same for other people in your personal life or your work.

The four types are:
- the German Shepherd, which has parallels to the person high in dominance in the DISC system and to the red personality in the red, blue, yellow and green system. This dog might also have parallels with the extrovert and thinker in the Myers-Briggs system.

- the Pomeranian, which has parallels to the person high in influence in the DISC system and the yellow personality in the red, blue, yellow and green system. This dog might have parallels with the extrovert and feelers in the Myers-Briggs system.

- the Golden Retriever, with parallels to the person high in steadiness in the DISC system and to the green personality in the red, blue, yellow, and green system. This dog might have parallels with the introvert and feeler in the Myers-Briggs system.

- the Border Collie, with parallels to the person high in conscientiousness in the DISC system or the blue personality in the red, blue, yellow, and green system. This dog might have parallels with the introvert and thinker in the Myers-Briggs system.

The 4 Dog Type Profiles reflect the different qualities of these four types of dogs.

The following chapters describe these four types in more depth so you can decide which one best fits you and the other people you are dealing with in your personal life or work, though the focus here is using this approach in the business-work environment.

Later chapters will deal with applying those personality types to create better relationships in your business and at work with customers, clients, co-workers, and employees.

PART I: HOW THE DOG TYPE SYSTEM WORKS

CHAPTER 1: RECOGNIZING THE FOUR DOG TYPES

As previously noted, the four key dog-types are these:

- The German Shepherd, who is the strong, aggressive leader. This is the person who thinks quickly, wants to get to the point, and makes fast decisions.

- The Pomeranian, which is very lively, outgoing, and loves excitement, variety, and change. He or she is a true extrovert and enjoys being the center of attention.

- The Golden Retriever, who is a warm, feeling, friendly person. He or she likes getting along with others, is calm and steady, and makes a good follower and team player.

- The Border Collie, who is thoughtful and analytical. He or she is interested in knowing the facts and taking time to reflect on and analyze them to make a careful decision.

Following is a little more about these four types of dogs, as described in more detail in *What's Your Dog Type?* and *Discovering Your Dog Type.*

Are You a German Shepherd?

A Little Bit of History…
     If you think of yourself or others as a German Shepherd, you picked a dog known for its strength and courage, as well as being a popular police dog.
     The German Shepherd was developed in Germany in the 1800s to herd and guard sheep. In 1899, the Verein fur Deutsche Scharferhunde SV was formed to improve the breed, so it not only made a great herding dog, but could be very courageous, athletic, and intelligent, making it an ideal police dog. It became a war sentry during WWI. For a time, its name was changed, so it wouldn't be associated with its roots in Germany, but in 1931, its original name was restored. It gained movie fame as Rin Tin Tin from the silent movie first released in 1922 and then produced as a films series and TV series, including a 1947 film with child actor Robert Blake and the 1950s TV series *The Adventures of Rin Tin Tin*. It has since been a popular police dog and has helped in search and rescue operations and detecting explosives, as well as being a popular pet.

What's Your Personality and Style?
     The German Shepherd type tends to have **lots of energy**, and is very **alert, intelligent, and serious.** If you are like a German Shepherd, you can be **stand-offish** when you first meet someone, and tend to be **strong,** even **domineering**. You are very **protective** of those you are close to, and are very **devoted** and **faithful**. You have a strong sense of **mission** or **purpose.**

Are You a Pomeranian?

A Little Bit of History...

If you think of yourself or others as a Pomeranian, you picked a catlike Toy Dog, that makes a great companion.

The Pomeranians are descendants of the Nordic sled dogs and at one point they were sheep dogs before they were recognized in their diminutive form in the 1870s as a pet and show dog. It is believed they were miniaturized in Germany, particularly in Pomerania, where they got their name. Their popularity spread after Queen Victoria brought a Pomeranian home from Italy, and they were bred in her royal kennels.

What's Your Personality and Style?

The Pomeranian type has the characteristics of this small but **feisty** toy dog, that is **very alert, vivacious, joyful,** and brimming with **high-energy.** If you are like a Pomeranian, you are also very much the **extrovert**, a real **people-person,** who loves to be with others, and makes a **warm, loving, affectionate** companion. You're usually **obedient,** are **eager to please** others, and you spread your **love** and **affection** around. You love **looking good** and appreciate **good grooming,** and have a high confidence that comes with **knowing you look good**. In fact, your confidence sometimes gets you in trouble, since you're sometimes ready to challenge the "big dogs", using your **cleverness** to outwit and outplay.

Are You a Golden Retriever?

<u>A Little Bit of History…</u>

If you think of yourself or others as a Golden Retriever, you picked a dog known for being helpful and friendly.

The Golden Retriever is a sporting dog which is among the most popular family dogs.

Golden Retrievers were developed in Scotland and England in the early 1800s to help with retrieving game from the water as well as on land, and they came to the U.S. in the 1890s. They are especially known for their obedience, and have become popular as guide dogs for the blind, as well as good at detecting narcotics for the police, because of their sensitive smell ability.

<u>What's Your Personality and Style?</u>

The Golden Retriever type tends to be a **very affectionate, warm, outgoing, extroverted people-person,** with **lots of energy**, just like these dogs. If you are like a Golden Retriever, you are often **playful,** and can be very **charming,** but you're **down-to-earth,** even **humble** in your nature, not showy or ostentatious. You have an **optimistic, cheery** outlook, and are **loyal** and **devoted** to others. No wonder you are likely to be **popular** and enjoy **socializing** with others, just like these dogs.

Are You a Border Collie?

A Little Bit of History…
If you think of yourself or others as a Border Collie, you picked a dog known for being smart, obedient, and loyal.

Border Collies are herding dogs, known for their helpfulness, loyalty, and obedience. They trace back to the days of sheepherders, especially in Scotland. The 18th century Scottish poet Robert Burns celebrated them as a good and faithful dog.

What's Your Personality and Style?
The Border Collie type has a great **get-along** personality, as someone who likes being with others. If you are like a Border Collie, you tend to have a **gentle, mild-mannered** personality, and make a great **follower** and **team player,** because you like to **go along** with what others are doing. You are eager to **please, take directions,** and are good at **following orders.** You tend to be a **very affectionate, loyal,** and **devoted** toward those you know and trust, though you may be more **reserved** with those you don't know very well.

CHAPTER 2: THE ROOTS OF THE DOG TYPE SYSTEM AND WHY IT WORKS

If you are wondering, why should you trust this Dog Type system for understanding different personalities and applying them to improve relationships and gain more success in your work or business, the answer is simple. It's because the Dog Type System is based on a series of time-tested personality systems with millions of followers. It draws on these systems which divide up individuals into four basic personality categories and have applied them for many years.

A key difference is that the Dog Type system uses four popular dogs to represent these different categories, so it makes using the system memorable and fun. Then, the book adds a variety of exercises and other activities that contribute to communicating with, persuading, working with, and managing others. In fact, the system is an approach where you can substitute in four different types of cats, other animals, cars, sports, whatever you want, to divide people into the four main personality categories – though this system is based on four very different dogs.

These long-standing personality systems which have inspired the Dog Type system include: the Myers-Briggs personality types, the DISC personality profiles, and the color profiling system.

So let me briefly describe these three systems and the qualities associated with the four major personality types.

The Myers-Briggs Type Indicator

The Myers-Briggs Type Indicator, also known as the MBTI, has a long history, going back to 1917, though the indicator was first published in 1944, and became the Myers-Briggs Type Indicator in 1956. It is based on a self-report questionnaire in which people's psychological preferences are determined by how they perceive the world and make decisions.

According to this theory, there are 16 types based on four preferences, and you are categorized according to your choices on these four dimensions. These are whether you prefer to deal with:
- people and things (Extraversion or "E") or ideas and information (Introversion or "I")
- facts and reality (Sensing or "S") or possibilities and potential (Intuition or "N")
- logic and truth (Thinking or "T") or values and relationships (Feeling or "F")
- a well-structure lifestyle (Judgment or "J") or going with the flow (Perception or "P").

In the Myers-Briggs system, you indicate your preference for one style over the other to get your personality type, such as ENTJ, if you are more extraverted, intuitive, thinking, and judgmental.

To determine your type, you take a test with 93-forced choice questions which represent opposite preferences on the same dichotomy. These questions involved choosing between different word pairs, or responding with a yes or no to a short statement. Then, your score indicates your preference on each of the four dichotomies, resulting in the 16 types once all of the possible choices are combined. However, even if you have a certain personality type, you still use all of the styles.

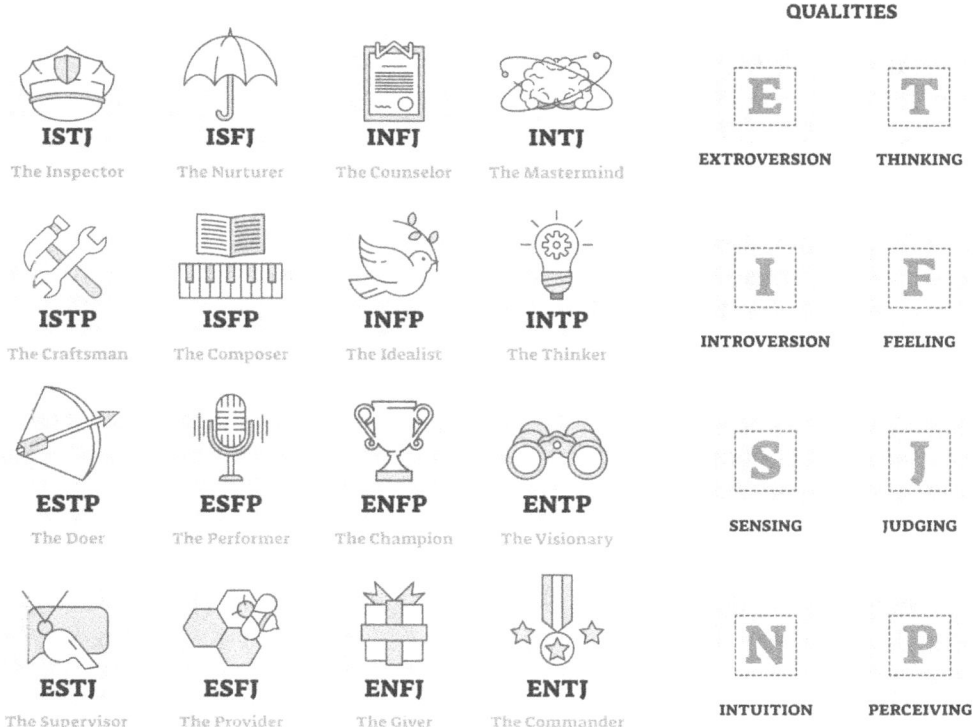

The Myers-Briggs system draws on the thinking about psychological types developed by the famous Swiss-German psychologist and psychologist Carl Gustav Jung, who founded analytical psychology. However, Jung only distinguished four cognitive functions – thinking, feeling, sensation, and intuition, resulting in eight types when combined with extraversion and introversion.

Myers-Briggs added the fourth category of judgment or perception. The basic theory is that one function is the most dominant and emerges early in life. Then, a second or auxiliary function emerges in one's teenage years and helps to balance the dominant. Later, in mid-life, a third or tertiary function develops, while the fourth or inferior function is least developed, and is more associated with the unconscious, so it comes out more frequently in situations of high stress.

Yet, despite the system's long-acceptance, it accuracy can easily be questioned, since it is based on self-reporting. As a result, anyone taking this test can manipulate the system to change the outcome – or one can easily select which description is most fitting without taking the test. Also, raising questions about the system's accuracy is the finding that over the years, researchers have found that only the I-E scale seems to have a high correlation with scales on other instruments. Additionally, the test is not always reliable, in that classifications can change when people take the test at different times.

In any event, the Myers-Briggs system is still widely used, and it is a highly complicated system. However, these 16 types can easily be reduced to the four types that are popularized, if you combine the Thinking and Feeling category with Judgment and Perception, and combine Extraversion and Introversion with Sensing and Intuition.

The first MBTI Manual was published in 1962; eventually it was published by the Consulting Psychologists Press in 1975, and the Center for Applications of Psychological Type (CAPT) was founded as a research laboratory to do studies on the system. The Association for Psychological Type International (APTI) was founded in 1979. An update of the manual was published in 1985, and a third edition was published in 1998.

I went to several meetings of the Psychological Type Association in the 1980s, and based on the results of the tests, people got into groups and discussed various topics; then they all joined together to share their experiences in the smaller groups. The idea of these exercises was to demonstrate how people in different groups not only had different attitudes towards the topic but had discussions and reached conclusions in different ways. There was also some discussion about the percentage of people who were in different categories based on their occupations, college majors, and country.

In short, the Myers-Briggs Type indicator is a personality system with a long history, and it includes some dichotomies that can be comparable to the four categories used in more recent personality systems, which have also contributed to creating the Dog Type and Cat Type systems.

The DISC Personality Profile

The DISC system also has a long history which goes back to the time of the ancient Greeks. In 444 BC, Empedocles identified the four elements – water, air, earth, and fire.

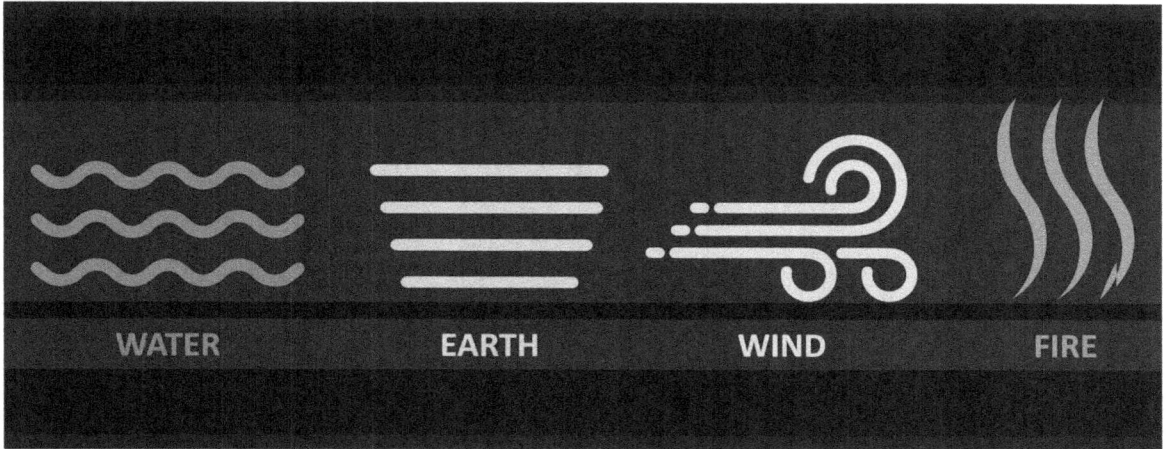

Then, and in 370 Hippocrates described the four basic substances or "humors" that made up the body -- blood, phlegm, yellow bile and black bile, while Galen, a Greek physician who lived from 129-217 A.D. in the Roman Empire, built on this theory to use opposites in treating illnesses. He also described the four temperaments as sanguine, phlegmatic, choleric, and melancholic. According to these early doctors, a balance of the four bodily fluids was required to maintain one's health. In effect, the four elements were turned into bodily fluids or humors, and supposedly one's dominant humor determined one's personality type. Based on those systems, there were the following associations:
- Water was related to being calm or phlegmatic, associated with phlegm,
- Air was related to being cheerful or sanguine, associated with blood,
- Fire was related to being enthusiastic or choleric, associated with yellow bile,
- Earth was related to being somber or melancholic, associated with black bile.

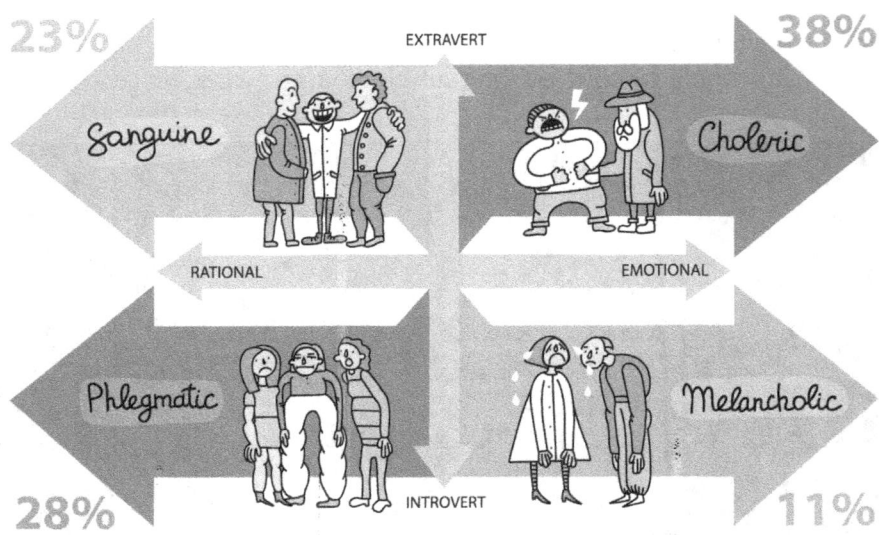

TEMPERAMENT INFOGRAPHICS

In 1921, Jung published his book *Psychological Types,* identifying the four ways of experiencing the world through sensation, feeling, intuition, and thinking that contributed to the Myers-Briggs theory.

Soon after that in 1928, the DISC system began when William Moulton Marston, a graduate in the newly developing field of psychology at Harvard University published his book *Emotions of Normal People.* According to this book, people had different styles of behavior that were developed through both internal influences and the environment. He identified four dimensions or styles of behavior which he characterized as D for dominant, I for influential, S for steady, and C for conscientious, although he noted that there were no pure styles; rather all people shared these styles in varying degrees of intensity.

In his view, the individuals with each DISC style had the following characteristics, indicated by the first term, whereas the second term is what is used in the system now.

Dominance/Dominant (D) – direct, decisive, high ego strength, problem solver, risk taker, self-starter

Inducement/Influential (I) – enthusiastic, trusting, optimistic, persuasive, talkative, impulsive, emotional

Submission/Steady (S) – good listener, team player, possessive, steady, predictable, understanding

Compliance/Conscientious (C) – accurate, analytical, conscientious, fact-finder, systematic, high standards.

A decade later, in 1940, Walter Clark built on Marston's theories to create the first DISC Personality Profile Report, and in the 1970s, John Geier used Clark's Self-Description to create the Personal Profile System, using hundreds of clinical interviews to expand upon the 15 basic patterns discovered by Clark by combining these four basic qualities. These include whether you are an achiever, agent, appraiser, counselor, creative, developer, inspirational, investigator, objective thinker, perfectionist, persuader, practitioner, promoter, results-oriented, or a specialist. A number of publishers have created their own versions of the DISC assessment tool.

But to get back to the basic four-part system, it provided a simple way to develop these personality profiles. This contributed to its rapid spread, because it was so easily learned and understood, although it can become more complicated when one combines one primary, secondary, and tertiary styles to create 40 DISC styles.

To learn how you rate, you can take an online DISC test in about 10 to 15 minute, or it takes about 15-20 minutes to complete a paper test. The assessment is supposed to be accurate from culture to culture, although different cultures may differently value different personality qualities, and one's style can change due to different situations or environments and can be affected by stress or change over time.

While the MBTI is still widely used today and can be used with the DISC system for a more in-depth, multi-faceted understanding at human behavior, the DISC system has grown in popularity. So now it has been used by over 50 million people since 1972, especially in business.

The DISC popularity is due to a number of reasons. Compared to the MBTI, it is less complicated and easier to understand and remember. A DISC test takes about half the time to complete, since it contains only 24 questions compared to about 90 questions on the MBTI test. It can be understood more easily without any training or guidance, and it takes less time for a person to become trained and certified in DISC theory and application. The system also focuses more on application than on theory compared to the MBTI system, and it emphasizes predictable behaviors - why we act and react as we do, whereas the MBTI focuses more on how we think internally based on our behavioral styles.

For example, one organization, Eastern Nazarene College that uses DISC assessments to help individuals become better leaders, lists a number of behavior indicators or common characteristics to look for in each of the behavioral styles.

- <u>The Dominant personality</u> tends to shape the environment and overcomes opposition to achieve the results. He or she is motivated by winning, competition, and success. He or she also tends to speak loudly, may interrupt others, and is poor at reading emotions. He or she sends very direct emails, too. Some other behaviors associated with the dominant personality according to PeopleKeys, one of the organizations that does DISC assessments, include these:
- emphasizes accomplishing results and is very confident
- sees the big picture
- can be blunt
- accepts challenges
- gets straight to the point

- The Influential personality tends to shape the environment by influencing or persuading others. He or she is motivated by social recognition, group activities, and relationships. He or she tends to turn work events into social gatherings, is eager to talk and jumps around from subject to subject. He or she commonly takes too much time to express a point to others, too. Some of the behaviors associated with the influential type according to PeopleKeys, include these:
- emphasizes influencing or persuading others, values openness and good relationships
- shows enthusiasm
- is optimistic
- likes to collaborate
- dislikes being ignored.

- The Steady personality emphasizes cooperating with others in the existing environment to attain one's goals. He or she is motivated by cooperation, by opportunities to help others, and by others' appreciation. He or she is an excellent listener, not highly expressive and has calm demeanor. He or she also tends to avoid topics which aren't familiar. Some of the behaviors associated with the steady type of personality according to PeopleKeys include these:
- emphasizes cooperation, sincerity, and dependability
- doesn't like to be rushed
- has a calm manner and approach
- offers supportive actions to others.

- The Conscientious personality works very conscientiously in the existing environment to make sure everything is of good quality and accurate. He or she is motivated by opportunities to gain knowledge, show expertise, and do quality work. He or she prefers to avoid small talk and asks many detail-oriented questions. Often he or she may make notes of these conversations to use later. Some of the behaviors associated with the conscientious personality according to PeopleKeys include these:
- emphasizes quality, accuracy, expertise, and competency
- enjoys independence
- employs objective reasoning
- wants the details
- doesn't like and fears being wrong

The DISC system is thus designed to use the knowledge of individual characteristics to better communicate with and motivate each person, if one is a leader or manager. It can also be used to better work with others or motivate them to become a client or customer.

An underlying premise of the DISC system is that all people are a blend of all four styles and all are equally valuable, though some people are higher in some styles than others. Thus, it can be helpful to consider one's primary, secondary, tertiary, and even absent style traits to better understand how others will act, react, communicate, work together, and deal with conflict.

Moreover, all of these styles are influenced by a variety of factors, including one's life experiences, education, and age.

     A first step to using the system and becoming more effective when you work with others is to better understand yourself. Then, you can use this knowledge to build more effective relationships. In particular, you can better understand others' priorities and how they differ from your own, so you can adapt your approach to better suit their style. Accordingly, as many who have used the system have found, the system is an effective method to improve one's personal and work relationships with others in these ways:

    - better work together in teams
    - have better relationships with friends, family members, and realtives
    - improve the productivity of teams
    - increase the ability of those in sales and customer service
    - contribute to change and conflict management
    - help with making decisions about hiring, recruiting, and promotion
    - become better at counseling and coaching
    - develop skills of management, supervision, and leadership
    - manage stress
    - better respond to the needs of clients and customers.

The Red-Blue-Yellow-Green Personality Type

Finally, a popular color test for personality styles is used in various forms today. These color choice tests offer various ways to determine these four types and apply them, though these tests draw some influences from the Myers-Briggs and DISC systems. They provide one more building block in creating the Dog Type system.

Two early versions of this color approach were developed by David Keirsey and Roger Birkman, as described by Martha Beth Lewis in an article comparing the three systems.[1]

David Keirsey first wrote his book *Please Understand Me: Character and Temperament Types* with Marilyn Bates in 1984. In it, he briefly introduced the Myers-Briggs system; then he reduced their 16 personality types into 4 temperament types – Dionysian (freedom first), Epimethean (wants to be useful), Promethean (wants power) and Apollonial (searches for self). The book sold over 2 million copies. In 1998, he published a refined version: *Please Understand Me II: Temperament, Character, Intelligence* in which he added in the four types of intelligence – tactical, logistical, diplomatic, and strategic, whereby individuals differ in their interests and skills, and he included in this the Keirsey Temperament Sorter, then the most used personality inventor in the world. He included the Keirsey Four-Types Sorter, a questionnaire indicating one's basic temperament and one's second, third, and fourth choices.

Keirsey also assigned the four temperaments with colors, though now with more practical, behavior-oriented descriptions than in his first book. He called the temperaments the "Guardians" – yellow; "Artisans" – red, "Idealists" – green, and "Rationals" – blue. He then divided them into four subtypes, and whereas the Myers-Briggs system emphasized how people think and feel, Keirsey focused more on how people behave. This emphasis on behavior is why the color system, like the DISC system, has been especially of interest to the business community.

---

[1] http://www.marthabeth.com/Birkman_Kirsey_Myers-Briggs.html

Meanwhile, Roger W. Birkman built on the Myers-Briggs system with his own color approach to personality, which can readily be compared with the Keirsey types. Birkman wrote his book *True Colors*, which was published in 1995, and later he wrote *The Birkman Method: Your Personality at Work*, based on his approach that was published by Sharon Birkman Fink and Stephanie Capparell in 2013. In *True Colors,* Birkman includes a short questionnaire, and based on your answers, you are assigned to one of four quadrants and assigned a color. The emphasis is on how you approach a group task, because of your personality traits, rather than revealing your personality type.

Based on this system, the colors correspond to these characteristics:
- If you are a yellow, you like order and closure and like to work with facts, not theories.
- If you are a red, you don't care about unfinished projects, but still like to work with facts not theories.
- If you are a green, you are logical, like to see possibilities, and are also sensitive to others emotions.
- If you are a blue, you are logical and like to see possibilities, but aren't much interested in people's emotions.

Or to combine the Birkman and Keirsey systems, this is how the color types see the world.
- Keirsey's blue "Rationals" are Birkman's blue "idea-centered people."
- Keirsey's yellow "Guardians" are Birkman's yellow "procedure-centered" people.
- Keirsey's red "Artistans" are Birkman's red "production-centered" people.
- Keirsey's green "Idealists" are Birkman's green "people-centered people."

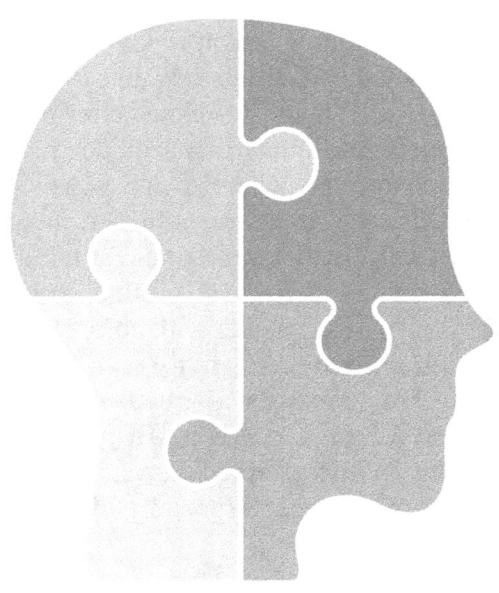

This history of how personality testing evolved may sound very complicated, but this is the root of the red-yellow-green-blue color system, which has morphed in various ways, and has many parallels with the DISC system. These influences, in turn, have gone into creating the 4 Dog Type system, which add a fun, modern variation on how to understand the different personality types and how they behave.

Some Modern Variations on the Red-Blue-Yellow-Green System

Today, you can find all sorts of red, blue, yellow, or green personality systems with various approaches to determining one's type. You will find some inconsistencies in associating a color with particular traits, although red is always the strong, dominating type. But the basic idea of distinguishing the four main types of people remains.

The College Morris Approach

College Morris, a marketer and business coach with a home business mainly in the U.K.[2] distinguishes the four types thus:

<u>Reds</u> are "strong leaders, fast-paced thinkers, risk takers, purposeful drivers, strong-willed, less patient, obvious energy, formal overtly competitive, rational." They are often leaders who take risks and are purposeful and confident. So when they interact with others, they like to feel in control and get to business quickly. They like others to be succinct and precise, give them facts, avoid detail, and talk about results and outcomes, so they can make quick decisions. They think and tend to move quickly.

<u>Yellows</u> are in essence party animals, since they are sociable, expressive, very imaginative, enthusiastic, very informal, very optimistic and animated. They are very relationship-focused and have high energy. The key to interacting with them is to socialize before you mention any business. They enjoy talking about other people. So you should be enthusiastic, energetic, and fast-paced when talking to them, and it helps to use humor and acknowledge their input when you talk.

<u>Blues</u> are the more serious types, who are deep thinkers, analytical, detail focused, and formal in their thinking. They sometimes may seem aloof. They have a deliberate approach, and they are systematic, precise, and pay attention to detail. They like things in their place, and are very organized with good time management skills. They like to come to their own conclusions, take time in their thinking, and are much slower-paced than reds or yellows. Sometimes they come across as perfectionists due to their logical, systematic, precise, and deliberate approach to problems or solutions. They like to have all the facts and then logically find a suitable answer. So when you deal with the blues, it's important to be well prepared, go into detail with the facts, and be logical in your approach. They like others to listen carefully to what they say, and they need time to respond since they think more slowly, and they like others to be formal and business-like in their approach.

Finally, <u>greens</u> tend to be cool, laid-back, relaxed, and patient. They are easy to get along with and very informal in their approach. They are social and focus on relationships they may come across as emotional. They also are slower-paced in their thinking and are very democratic. In interacting with others, they like people to be friendly, show a genuine interest in them, and chat for a while before getting down to business. They like to develop trust first, and they like to keep things informal and non-threatening.

Yet, while everyone may have a dominant personality style, everyone is a mix of all the colors.

---

[2] http://www.evancarmichael.com/library/colette-morris/Are-you-a-Red-Blue-Yellow-or-Green-Personality-Type.html

The MJ Gruesso Approach

Another take on the four color system is provided by M.J. Gruesso, a psychologist[3] Theses color types are characterized as follows:

Reds – these are the dominating personality. They like things to be done their way and right now. They like getting immediate results, making quick decisions, and are persistent in whatever they do. They like to solve problems, take charge, appear self-reliant, and accept challenges. They like new and varied activities and getting things done. They like being in control over the situation and want direct answers from others. Their weaknesses are that they can sometimes be impatient and insensitive to others, and they can be inflexible and demanding. At times they may be inattentive to details and don't like restrictions.

Yellows – these are the life of the party types. They tend to be happy-go-lucky, turn to friends if under stress, and want acceptance from others, so they most fear others' rejection. They tend to be very optimistic and enthusiastic, like to help others, and create an entertaining climate. They like a friendly warm environment, seek public recognition of their ability, love to talk, want positive reinforcement, and like freedom from control. They tend to be weak in follow-through and may overestimate their results, act impulsively before thinking, and jump to conclusions.

Greens – these are the calm personality types, who don't get easily frazzled or upset, even under stress. They like to maintain harmony, but sometimes get taken advantage of, because they don't like to say no. Then tend to be supportive, agreeable, loyal, and exercise good self-control. They are consistent, a good listener, and good at developing personal relationships. They like being appreciated, like security, and hope for minimal conflict between others. Their weaknesses include resisting change, being indecisive, being overly lenient with others, and lacking initiative.

Blues – these are the perfectionists, who like to examine the details of every situation. They can often seem unemotional, and they most fear being criticized. They tend to be very orderly, conscientious, disciplined, precise, thorough, and analytical. They like to concentrate on detail. They also like stable surroundings and procedures, enjoy planning; want sufficient time to get things right, and like exact descriptions and expectations for what they are supposed to do. Sometimes they can get bogged down in details and can be indecisive, because they want to look at all the data and are hesitant to try new things. They can be pessimistic and overly sensitive to criticism, too.

The Rainbow Personality Test

Still another approach to the four colors is the Rainbow Personality Test, translated by Mona Dahms, for a SAIL Course, which refers to Sustainability in International Learning offered by the Baltic University.[4]

---

[3] https://general-psychology.knoji.com/which-color-personality-are-you-red-blue-green-or-yellow
[4] http://www.balticuniv.uu.se/index.php/component/docman/cat_view/122-students/166-sail-2011

In this system, a test with 40 questions indicates a person's strengths and weaknesses in participating in team work. You answer by rating the questions on a scale from 1 (hardly ever/never true) to 5 (almost always true). Then, these scores for each statement are placed in 4 columns and graded on four axes to indicate your relative red, yellow, green, and blue scores. A short interpretation of the test echoes the other descriptions of the four colors with the following characterizations:

<u>Red</u>: Effective, optimistic, goal oriented, energetic, dominating, and hotheaded. Wants to be the best and to be successful.

<u>Yellow</u>: Lots of ideas, airy, flexible and impulsive. Doesn't like rules and procedures. Wants freedom.

<u>Blue</u>: Persistent, stable, and conscientious. Does not like to be criticized. Wants stability and safety.

<u>Green</u>: The bureaucrat. Likes order and stability. Good at sorting ideas and coordinating activities.

A Teacher's Approach with Students

To take one more example, this four colors approach was used by teachers to help students understand different personality types and better work with others in a group. Instead of a questionnaire, students were asked to circle one word or phrase per line that most described them or what they liked, such as if they were more self-confident, structured, sensitive, or trusting. Then, they were scored based on the number of their red, green, blue, or yellow choices for each item on the list. The result was a score for each color, indicating which was their dominant, next most dominant, and least dominant trait.

As for the characteristics of each color choice, they pretty much echoed what the other personality tests reflected, with one exception – the blue and green characteristics were switched. But with that caveat, here's how the personality types are described.

Reds: They are task and results oriented. They like recognition and tend to make good leaders. They love leadership roles and enjoy managing people.

Yellows: They are people-oriented, expressive, friendly, optimistic, and love to talk. They are generally outgoing and fun-loving. They are the glue that holds groups together.

Greens: They like order and keeping things organized.

Blues: They are often quiet, sometimes shy. Often they are the innovative, idea people, who tend to be independent loners.

Summing Up

So there you have it. The major four-color splits that are often comparable to the four-part DISC divisions and to some of the Myers-Briggs type categories.

CHAPTER 3: WHERE THE 4-DOG TYPE SYSTEM FITS

The 4-Dog Type system builds on 4-type personality systems that have gone before, most notably the Myers-Briggs, DISC, and the color profile systems.

How the Dog Type System Differs from Other Systems

The big difference from other personality systems lies in using Dog Types to represent different types of people. This approach consolidates the descriptions from these other systems and it simplifies the process of determining the type that represents you, since you don't have to answer questions or select words on a chart. You simply read over the descriptions and rate how much each description seems to fit you on a scale of 1-10, so you can quickly decide on your type.

Finally, and most importantly, using the Dog Types system makes the process fun and relatable, since millions of people own or love dogs. This system also provides a comfortable way to talk about personality differences in workshops or to better communicate and interact with others for different purposes – whether to improve your personal relationships, get more customers and clients, make more sales, or improve relationships in the workplace.

Why Choose the 4 Selected Dogs for the 4-Dog Type System

The particular dogs chosen to represent the four types were selected because they are among the most popular dogs that reflect these personality types. The four dogs selected are:
 the German Shepherd for the red or dominant (D) personality
 the Pomeranian for the yellow or influencer (I) personality
 the Golden Retriever for the green or calm, friendly, steady (S) personality (although this color is blue in some color systems)
 the Border Collie for the blue or conscientious (C) personality (although this color is green in some color systems)

However, the particular dogs selected could easily be changed if there are stronger associations with other dogs. For example:
 - The red or dominant personality could be represented by a Rottweiler or Pit Bull, since they have a reputation for being aggressive fighters.
 - The yellow or influencer personality could be represented by a Pug or Chihuahua, since they are very friendly, sociable dogs.
 - The green or steady personality could be represented by a Labrador or St. Bernard, since they have a very family-oriented and helper personality.

- The blue or conscientious personality could be represented by Siberian Huskies, since they are very intelligent dogs, though more independent and feisty than Border Collies.

In short, the most popular dog types have been selected for these personality profiles, although you can substitute other dogs with similar characteristics to represent the different types. With that, here are the characteristics of each dog type. You can use the following profile page to rate which type most characterizes you – and you can think about others you communicate or interact with in a similar way. Then, you can apply these distinctions to better communicate or interact with others.

The Key Characteristics of the Four Types of Dogs

The following chart summarizes the major characteristics associated with each type of dog. Notice which characteristics most describe you and rate each type from 1 to 10. Then, list the dogs from the highest to lowest.

The first two dogs with the highest ratings are the major ways in which you relate to the world; you might consider dogs with the highest ratings your Top Dog and Watch Dog. Consider your lowest rated dog your Underdog.

You can think of the people you know or meet using these Dog Type profiles, based on your impressions of what their personality is like. Later, as you get to know people better, you can revise the way you think of them based on a greater understanding of who they are.

THE FOUR DOG TYPES

German Shepherd (Red-Dominant)	Pomeranian (Yellow-Influencer)	Golden Retriever (Green – Steady)	Border Collie (Blue – Conscientious)
Results-oriented Success-motivated Goals-driven A leader Competitive Direct Confident Accepts challenges Fast-paced thinker Risk taker Strong-willed Purposeful Like facts quickly Avoids detail Interested in results Decisive	Enthusiastic Optimistic Values good relationships Collaborative Likes attention and appreciation Persuasive People person Sociable Expressive Life of the party Enjoys humor Seek acceptance	Likes cooperation Seeks sincerity, dependability Calm manner Supportive Cool Laid-back Relaxed Not easily upset Patient Social Friendly Interest in others Easy-Going Values trust Can be indecisive Likes security	Perfectionist Detail-oriented Orderly Organized Conscientious Disciplined Precise Analytical Likes stability Likes planning and procedures Sensitive to criticism Wants to get things right

Now rate yourself from 1-10 for each type:
German Shepherd (red-dominant) _____
Pomeranian (yellow-influencer) _____
Golden Retriever (green-steady) _____
Border Collie (blue-conscientious) _____

How do you rate your types (if any ties, choose one for a higher rating):
    Dominant Type (Top Dog) _____
    Next Strongest Type (Watch Dog) _____
    Lowest Ranked Type (Underdog) _____

    Now that you have a better sense of your own personality, based on your favorite, next favorite, and least favorite dog type, you can imagine what others are like, when you first meet or get to know them. You can modify your assessment of their personality type as you further interact with and learn more about them.

The following chapters will show you how to apply this knowledge about your type and that of others in various situations from your friends and family to getting customers and clients to managing others or working together. The last chapter features a sample workshop you can use with associates or others in your organization to apply these techniques to achieving your main goals in using these Dog Types, such as to improve your relationship with a significant other, build your business, or improve your workplace relationships.

PART II: APPLYING THE DOG TYPE SYSTEM

CHAPTER 4: UNDERSTANDING YOUR STRENGTHS AND WEAKNESSES

Before considering how to better relate to others based on their personality type, it is good to recognize your own weaknesses or areas of improvement, based on your Dog Type. This way you might consider how to modify your approach, especially when you encounter someone of a different personality type – or even the same type, if your approaches are likely to clash.

When Strengths Can Help

At times, your strengths can be the perfect fit for the occasion. Say you're a German Shepherd and your organization needs a strong leader to steer it through uncertain times. Or maybe you're a part of a group that's vacillating over making choices and deciding on goals. A German Shepherd with a clear vision about what to do can persuade others to act in a certain way and guide them on the path. Or as a German Shepherd, you may be persuasive in convincing a customer to buy a more expensive model that he really wants rather than choosing a less expensive and less desired choice for practical reasons. Or to take a personal situation, you might need to make a decision and support it about what to do in a conflict between family members.

Alternatively, suppose an organization has been wracked by conflicts between members, or maybe a customer is irate because she feels she was misled into buying something or feels insulted by something a salesperson has said. A Golden Retriever green/steady type might be just the type of person to calm things down and bring harmony back to the group. For instance, the Golden Retriever might sit down with the aggrieved person, listen for a while, and come up with a fair solution to help the upset person feel better. Or the Golden Retriever might help a group wracked with conflict overcome differences to find a solution that brings about harmony. Or in a personal situation, you might need to play a supportive, helper role to soothe hard feelings in a family conflict.

Or say you are a Pomeranian yellow/influencer type. Maybe you can help motivate everyone to give them a reason to work together again. You might talk about the great things the group has accomplished in the past, or the group's potential to be great again. You might cheer everyone on with a group song or put together a fun party, so everyone feels there a new purpose for the group. You can be the life of the party in family gatherings or in get-togethers with friends.

Or what if you are a Border Collie blue/conscientious type? You might take some time to think about what the group needs going forward and draw up some plans with timelines and goals. You might talk to people in the group to find out what each person wants. Then, you might have a meeting where you share these ideas in order to come up with a balanced slate of plans that provide a little bit of what everyone wants. In this way, you can become a kind of great compromiser to bring everyone together. Or in your family, you can be a great record keeper, who keeps track of the household finances or be a excellent planners for family celebrations.

Thus, at times your strengths can be very useful, and you and others can benefit, when you know how and when to use them in a particular situation.

When Strengths Become Weaknesses

Sometimes your strengths can turn into weaknesses, when they don't fit the situation or make matters even worse.

For example, suppose you are a German Shepherd type, with a red or dominant personality, so you are apt to come on very strong, as you exercise your leadership role or seek to dominate a conversation. But in some situations, that's not a good idea. One scenario is where you are not the leader, but are working with a team leader or boss. If you become too bossy, you may upset the designated leader, who sees you as a threat. Or in a personal relationship, a friend or mate may see you as being too controlling. Then, depending on the other person's personality style, you may experience several different things.

If the other person is also a German Shepherd type, he or she may be more likely to confront you to put you in your place, though the form that confrontation takes could vary depending on the situation. A boss, for instance, might yell you down, insult you in front of your peers, or fire you, because German Shepherds tend to be more aggressive and combative. A mate or sibling could become angry and resistant and fight back.

If the other person is a Border Collie type, which has a blue or conscientious personality, he or she may be more likely to quietly work behind the scenes to get back at you for your usurpation or plan something devious. For instance, a Border Collie boss might give you more work, so you have to work longer hours each day or have to give up a weekend. Or perhaps the boss might give you more difficult work, so you are likely to make mistakes. Then, you have to abjectly humiliate yourself to get back in the boss's good graces, or he or she now has a reason to fire you. In a personal relationship, a friend or mate might be devious and quietly act without sharing information with you, so they get what they want without risking a negative response from you.

If the other person is a Pomeranian, the yellow influencer, who enjoys being the life of the party, such a boss might use your challenge to authority as an opportunity to put you on the hot seat, so you are humiliated in front of others and avoid any more challenges to your boss. It is as if your boss sets a trap to have fun at your expense like a circus ring master, where you are the clown. Or say you have organized a family gathering. The Pomeranian type might do something to become the center of attention, from grabbing the mic to leading a line dance, so attendees remember that, not your hard work in putting together the event.

Or say your boss is a Golden Retriever, the calm green steady type who likes things to go smoothly and hopes everyone can get along. He or she might call you in to talk about what just happened and ask you to be more collaborative and cooperative in the future. In this way, he or she might use shaming, but in private, so you will learn to accept that your boss has more power, and you know not to challenge him or her in the future. Finally, in a personal situation, the

Golden Retriever type might try to smooth over a relationship after you have angrily put down someone in the family by acting as a kind of mediator to quell any disagreement.

Of course, how other people react in any situation may vary, though knowing or assessing their personality style can help you expect them to reacting to the way you have acted, based on your personality type. While your type will have certain strengths, such as if your company or family needs your leadership style, at other times your type could be a weakness, if you don't recognize or learn to control how you express your natural tendencies based on your type. Thus, it is important to recognize the type of weaknesses you might exhibit, so you are better able to control them.

Accordingly, the following sections illustrate the types of strengths and weaknesses to be aware of, depending on your dominant type. As this discussion of different patterns illustrates, whatever your type, you should be aware of both your strengths and weaknesses, so you can better balance them. Additionally, through this awareness, you can better know what qualities to assert at different times. This knowledge can also indicate where you might want to improve in order to have better relationships and thereby more success in achieving whatever you want.

What If You're a German Shepherd?

As a German Shepherd, you tend to be strong in leadership qualities, such as being assertive, powerful, and dominant. You like to take charge, get results, and win at whatever you do. You can be very good as a leader when you have the power and you take others interests and needs into consideration, no matter the situation.

For example, in a sales situation, you can first learn what the person needs and wants. Then, you can use that information to guide that person into making a purchase by showing the value of that purchase. Or as a company owner or manager, you can do some fact gathering to decide what to do in a particular situation – such as whether to make an acquisition or expand the company through more aggressive marketing. Once having made that decision, you can persuade your people that this is a good strategy to make the company even stronger, thereby leading to more productivity and loyalty. Or as a member of a work team or organization, you can volunteer to lead some committee, inspire others to join with you, and lead the group to complete the task successfully. Or in a personal situation, you can take the lead in making decisions about what to do or where to go.

But at times, your qualities can turn into weaknesses and alienate others, because you exercise these qualities at the wrong times or too abrasively. For example, at a meeting, you may speak too loudly, interrupt other speakers, or dominate the floor with too many questions or comments. Or you may be too direct and forceful, so you come across as tactless or domineering. Then, too, in your drive to get results, you may come across as too impatient and insensitive. Other weaknesses are that you can overlook risks, be inflexible, and demand too much of others. In a conversation, you might talk too much or you might be inattentive to details, because you want to move too quickly to achieve results. And you might inappropriately push through restrictions.

Thus, it's important to notice others' reactions to you to see if you are coming on too strong or acting in other ways that might be off-putting. Some ways to notice a negative reaction to you is if people seem to be withdrawing from you, disregarding what you are asking them to do, tuning you out, or hesitating to share their disagreement, since they seem afraid of you.

More specifically, some of your weaknesses or areas for improvement include these:
- Being insensitive towards others
- Being too direct, so you seem rude, insulting, or unkind
- Poor at reading others' emotions
- Being impatient
- Overlooking risks
- Being inflexible
- Being overly demanding of others
- Talking too much or speaking too loudly at times
- Interrupting others
- Being inattentive to details
- Resenting and resisting restrictions

Some ways to overcome these negatives include being more aware of what others are thinking and feeling, listening more, slowing down, taking more personal time, or taking more time to relax. When appropriate, you might invite others to lead, and give or share credit when this is due.

What If You're a Pomeranian?

If you are a Pomeranian, with a yellow or influencer personality, you are a great people person. You love to be around others, and are full of enthusiasm and energy. You enjoy the attention and appreciation of others, and you are great at influencing and persuading people to do things. You also like to keep things fun and exciting.

These qualities can be great at meetings, since you are good at keeping things interesting. You attract people who love to be around you because of your optimistic exuberant personality. Such qualities can work wonders in many sales situations, since you can inspire and influence people to get on board because whatever product or service you are selling seems to be great. And as a speaker or seminar leader, you can be a great motivator and inspirational leader.

These qualities can also work well if you are a company owner or manager in certain fields, where you want to keep people revved up and raring to go, such as in a company involved in sales, recreation, and hospitality. As a team leader in a company, you can contribute to the team's good morale and productivity by making whatever you do fun, such as coming up with an incentive contest to motivate people to do more. Or you can spice up a barbecue or party with family and friends.

But at other times, your qualities can turn into negatives. For instance, since you are motivated by social recognition, group activities, and relationships, you may turn work activities into overly social gatherings, so you interfere with the purpose of the group. Everyone may have a lot more fun at work, but they may become less productive, so the organization may lose its focus on achieving certain goals. Another problem is an emphasis on keeping things interesting and fun can lead you and the group members to lose focus. You and any people you are leading may be more likely to jump from subject to subject, which can undermine results. Then, too, you may be more apt to ramble and take too much time to get your point across, unlike the more direct, "just the facts" approach of the German Shepherd. And with family members and friends you may fail to take a difficult situation seriously enough by offering lighthearted comments or trying to change the subject to a more entertaining topic.

More specifically, some of your weaknesses or areas for improvement include these:
- Turning business and work activities into more fun social gatherings, which undermine productivity (in contrast to using fun activities to motivate and inspire)
- Losing focus as you shift your attention from one thing to another
- Being overly informal and humorous, when the situation requires more formality and gravitas
- Not following through, because you don't like detail or are on to the next subject
- Overestimating results and misjudging capabilities, because you imagine the possibilities, rather than paying attention to the steps for getting to a goal and realistically assessing if you really have the abilities to get there
- Talking too much, because you enjoy being the center of attention
- Acting impulsively and jumping to conclusions, because you are more interested in the big picture and how you imagine things to be, not how they are
- Acting first and thinking second, because that's your style
- Overcommitting yourself, your company, or your group, because you want to get along and be appreciated, and you don't like to say no
- Taking too much time to get to the point, because you are too involved in making the process enjoyable, rather than focusing on what needs to be done to achieve the desired results.

Some ways to overcome these negatives include being more results-oriented and following through to achieve those results, paying more attention to detail to realistically determine what is needed to achieve a particular goal, and taking the time to listen more. You should also hold back your desire to quickly act or draw conclusions, so you can get more facts and accurately assess the situation. Additionally, you can talk less, listen more, and be ready to say no, if you feel you are overcommitted or can't do a particular tasks. Then, too, if you would rather not be a leader and would rather organize fun group activities, suggest someone else for a top leadership role and offer to participate in a more fun way, which is more in line with what you like to do and are good at doing. For instance, you might motivate everyone to do something and lead others in fun, invigorating activities, from a party to a great conference or retreat.

What If You're a Golden Retriever?

If you are a Golden Retriever with a green or calm and steady personality, you are great at encouraging harmony between others. Even at times of stress, you are like a beacon of steadiness, and you can help to keep the organization on an even keel, like a ship weathering a storm. You like cooperating with others and getting people to work together. You are also a great listener, so people can turn to you when they need help, and you are great at calming down people who are upset about something.

Such qualities can be great if people are showing uncertainty about anything, whether people in a company are dealing with challenges or prospective customers are deciding whether to buy something that requires new skills or is more expensive than their budget. You can be a good listener to encourage people to talk about their concerns, and you can provide reassurance for them, so they decide to take on some challenge or buy. Likewise, you can be a great sounding board and conciliator when people have conflicts. Then, you can help heal the breach by listening and getting people to compromise, much like a mediator acts as a neutral go-between to help people in a dispute work out the issue themselves, and does not take sides or tell others what to do.

Yet, at times such strengths can turn into negatives, when more assertive or creative responses are called for. For instance, it doesn't always work to have someone act as a neutral third party mediator, when others are having an argument. Sometimes it's necessary to take a more forceful stand, such as a German Shepherd type might determine what is the best action under the circumstances. Or maybe people need a break from dealing with the problem by participating in some fun activity that might end the log jam, such as might be suggested by a Pomeranian type. Or maybe some more facts and analysis, such as offered by the Border Collie type, might be what both sides need to see the issue more clearly in order to arrive at a reasonable solution.

Another negative is that at times your desire for stability and security can prevent needed change from occurring, and this resistance can hold a group or organization back. Perhaps your concern with being certain can lead you to be indecisive when a quick decision is needed. Or perhaps your desire to maintain good relations with everyone can lead you to be too accepting of people's flaws, which prevents you from seeing that someone is holding the group back and needs to be dismissed, not encouraged to do better, when that strategy hasn't worked in the past. In a family or with friends, this "let's all get along" approach can discourage real differences from being expressed and get resolved.

More specifically, some of your weaknesses or areas for improvement include these:
- not being assertive enough
- resisting or not being able to adapt to change
- being overly lenient with people
- being indecisive and procrastinating
- being overly slow-moving in working towards goals
- being too laid back and informal
- having trouble making deadlines
- lacking initiative
- having difficulty in saying no, so people can take advantage of you
- failing to recognize when someone or something is bad for an organization or group, because of a desire to maintain harmony
- trusting too much or remaining loyal to an individual or organization that is making mistakes or engaged in wrongful acts.

Some ways to overcome these negatives include asserting yourself more, being open to change, and being more critical of people and organizational activities. Work on becoming more decisive and goal oriented, too. And as appropriate, become more formal in the way you relate to others, and be more ready to say no, when someone asks you to do something or support something, which you don't want to do or support.

What If You're a Border Collie?

If you're a Border Collie with a blue or conscientious personality, you are great at paying attention to details, and you are motivated by the opportunity to gain knowledge, show off your expertise, and do quality work. You love knowing the facts and keeping everyone informed about the current situation. You are great at helping to gather research to support a point you or someone else in an organization is making. You are also ideally suited to guide people in making the best choices based on the way things are or helping to make a detailed plan to achieve a future possibility.

Such qualities can be great if someone is organizing a new company and needs a business plan to show why this is a good investment. These qualities are also ideal in a sales situation when a prospect wants hard facts to be convinced on making a major purchase, such as a car, especially if the buyer also has a Border Collie personality. This conscientious approach also works well if a document requires detailed facts and documentation, such as a legal brief, an investigative report, or an application for a grant. This approach is also ideal if you are taking courses or preparing for exams on any subject. Or if you are trying to persuade others to do something, the stats prepared by a Border Collie can contribute to a compelling PowerPoint presentation or speech. You can help by keeping the financial and tax records for your family.

But there are other times when the strengths of the Border Collie type can turn into negatives. For example, you might find yourself overloaded by seeking to get the facts right and not wanting to delegate, because you fear someone else will do it incorrectly. You may spend too much time away from others, so you don't participate in or enjoy social events. Or you may take so much time gathering all the facts that you delay making a decision for too long.

Another negative is that you may get so mired in details that you don't see the big picture. You may fail to be in touch with your intuition or gut, so you don't receive, ignore, or don't trust insights you get from any sources other than your reason – but at times your reason can be wrong, and your gut feelings can be right. Your concern with how things are in the present can lead you to avoid trying something new or thinking about the future. Thus, you may lack initiative or resist suggestions to improve, because you are too focused on how things are now. So like the Golden Retriever, who values stability, you may resist change out of your desire for security – or different reason, but the result is the same.

More specifically, some of your weaknesses or areas for improvement include these:

- Wanting to get *all* the facts, when you can use a sampling or sufficient number of facts to recognizing trends

- Being indecisive because you are waiting to get all the facts

- Looking only to your reason and not trusting or being in touch with your intuitive or gut-level feelings

- Getting bogged down in details

- Feeling low self-esteem, because you trust the facts but not yourself

- Being overly sensitive to criticism, because you want to be seen as knowledgeable, authoritative, and right

- Being hesitant to try new things, because you can't know what will happen, since the facts aren't there yet

- Avoiding controversy, because you want to make safe choices and don't want to rock the boat

- Being pessimistic, because you feel more comfortable with the way things are and feel uncertain about what the future may bring.

Some ways to overcome these negatives include being more ready to look beyond the facts to consider possibilities, being more decisive based on the data you have now, becoming more in touch with your feelings, and trusting your intuition and gut level feelings more. Some other things you might do to improve are to be more positive about the present and the future, and become more receptive to trying new things. Then, too, look for the big picture rather than getting bogged down in the details, and don't resist criticism. Instead, think about what you can learn from any criticism to do things better in the future.

CHAPTER 5: ASSESSING HOW TO BETTER COMMUNICATE WITH AND INTERACT WITH OTHERS BASED ON THEIR DOG TYPE

Once you know your own Dog Type, you will be more aware of your strengths and weaknesses and can better adapt your approach in communicating with others. Take into consideration the other party's type, so you can adjust your approach accordingly.

While you may not know the other person's Dog Type for sure, unless he or she tells you, you can make a likely assessment based on how that person comes across to you, when you first meet or have an extended conversation. Use the characteristics for the different Dog Types in figuring out where you and the other person fit.

You'll see a summary of the major characteristics to look for in the following chart. The more traits the person has, the higher he or she rates in having that as a dominant trait. While everyone is a combination of the four Dog Types, some types are more dominant than others in a person's personality. Generally, look for the person's dominant type and adapt your approach to that, whether you are seeking a customer, working together with a boss, trying to find a job, or getting to know someone in your personal life.

The chart on the following page highlights the major characteristics of each type. Next, I'll discuss how to adapt your approach to each type under varying circumstances.

DOG TYPE CHARACTERISTICS CHART

German Shepherd (Red/Dominant Type) The Leader	Pomeranian (Yellow/Influencer Type) The Fun Party Animal	Golden Retriever (Green/Steady Type) The Cool Supporter	Border Collie (Blue/Conscientious Type) The Serious Fact Checker
Strong leader	High energy, enthusiastic	Likes to help and support others	Conscientious, thorough
Has leadership skills	Expressive	Supportive	Perfectionist
Like being in control	Very animated	Interest in others	Very orderly, discipline, precise
Strong-willed	Very outgoing, sociable	Good listener	Well-organized
Wants to win, be the best	Fun loving, life of the party	Wants to cooperate, collaborate	Good time management skills
Seeks success	Often happy-go-lucky	Friendly, sociable	Likes planning, procedures
Goal-oriented	Enjoys good humor	Informal with others	Detail-oriented
Purposeful	Optimistic	Easy-going	Asks detail-oriented questions
Results-oriented	Likes good relationships	Patient	Wants accuracy, facts
Like immediate results	Relationship-focused	Normally calm, cool, collected	Logical, systematic, precise
Want to get things done	People person	Laid-back, relaxed	Uses objective reasoning
Very competitive	Likes social gatherings	Not easily upset	Analytical, deep thinker
Like challenges	Likes collaboration, collaborative	Readily adapts, adjusts	Likes coming to own conclusions
Willing to take risks, risk-taker	Loves to talk with others	Likes the familiar, comfortable	Concern with quality
Persistent	Seeks social recognition, praise, acceptance	Likes order, stability	Emphasizes competence
Optimistic	Enjoys attention, appreciation	Like keeping things organized	Wants to be right and get things right
Confident, self-assured	Most fears rejection	Good at coordinating activities	Doesn't like being wrong
Can make quick decisions, decisive	Seeks positive reinforcement	Sincere and trustworthy	Dislikes criticism
Likes getting straight to the point	Likes friendly, warm environment	Seeks sincerity, dependability	Likes to gain knowledge
Fast-paced thinker	Creates entertaining atmosphere	Values trust	Wants to show expertise
Likes facts quickly	Likes influencing/persuading	Dependable	Doesn't like small talk
Doesn't like details	Likes freedom from control		May seem aloof, reserved
Interested in big picture	Flexible		Can seem unemotional
	Doesn't like rules, procedures		Likes stability and safety
	May act impulsively		Quiet, sometimes shy
			Likes independence
			Often innovative, idea person
			Sometimes independent loners

Adapting Your Approach to Others

You can use the chart on the previous page to help you remember the characteristics of the different Dog Type personality, behaviors, and interests. Then, use the knowledge of these personality traits to help you vary your approach to sales, working together, managing or coordinating a team, seeking a job from different types of bosses, and having better relationships in your personal life.

I'll first describe how to adapt your approach in general and provide some examples from these different situations. Future books will go into more depth on how to best modify your approach in different settings.

In deciding how to best relate to someone, first consider the other person's Top Dog, or most usual traits and behaviors, in light of your preferences. Then, consider how these dominant traits might be modified by the person's next common traits and behaviors, which might be characterized as that that person's Watch Dog. An example of such an analysis is shown in the chart below at a workshop showing how different people vary in the strength of different traits.

Relating to the German Shepherd (Red/Dominant Leadership Type)

If you are dealing with a German Shepherd type, you are dealing with someone who is bottom-line, results-oriented, and wants the big picture. He or she is very interested in winning, success, achieving goals, and getting things done. Therefore, not only include some facts to support your point of view, but keep your presentation or meeting short and to the point.

You don't want to spend much time socializing or making small talk. Instead, quickly emphasize the benefits and don't get bogged down presenting the features or why something works. A few examples might be enough to support your point of view.

Also, since the German-Shepherd type sees him/herself as a leader, defer to his or her lead, should he or she ask any questions or ask for more information. In that case, provide more supporting evidence to make your case, though keep it brief and don't offer too much detail. In fact, this might be a good time to offer the supporting information in a handout or report. But preface any written material with a short executive-type summary or abstract with the main points – and perhaps include a few graphs, photos, and illustrations to make the point even more dramatically.

Some things to emphasize in a meeting or conversation are how the German Shepherd type can win and succeed using whatever you are offering, whether a product, service, new system, or hiring you for a job. Should there be some challenges or risks in taking on what you are proposing, mention them, but emphasize how he or she can overcome them and receive recognition and glory for succeeding, especially if the first to do something. Also, stress the likelihood of succeeding, and you believe that person has the skills to make success likely. Then, show how you can help the person win.

Importantly, emphasize the recognition and prestige the German Shepherd type will gain by doing whatever you are proposing. Should your proposal involve doing something for a good cause or helping others, mention that, but point up how others will look up to the person for taking action.

If you are a German Shepherd type yourself, you should be in your natural element in describing the project, the value of doing it, and how you can help to make it happen. However, don't go overboard in giving yourself credit, since then the German Shepherd type may then see you as a threat, because he or she likes being the leader – or "top dog."

So position yourself as a subordinate, right hand person, or wingman or woman. Show that you share similar values and goals in wanting to get things done and make things happen. And show that you are optimistic that the proposed activity will have a winning outcome. Point up your commitment to achieving the results. Emphasize that you are there to help the other person make things happen and that he or she will get the credit for supporting or advocating this project. Unless the other person proposes it, don't position yourself as being a partner or in charge, unless you are bringing some money to the table, and if so, point out how the other person will have a title to show that he or she is in charge, and you are providing support behind the scenes.

Taking into Consideration the German Shepherd's Secondary Type

In addition to considering the German's Shepherd's primary characteristics when you communicate, consider how to adapt your approach based on whether that person's second Dog Type is a Pomeranian, Golden Retriever, or Border Collie, and how important those qualities are to the person. For example, if a person is an out-and-out German Shepherd, who is very interested in dominance and power, these other qualities may be less important. Otherwise, these secondary choices may play an influential role, especially if another trait is a close second to the person's primary choice.

Here's how to adapt your approach for each one.

If the German Shepherd also has the qualities of a Pomeranian, that means he or she likes to have fun, too, so you might focus on doing business first, but then get ready to share some fun. Or if you are relating to a boss or seeking a job, talk about what you do for fun. You might also point up the social advantages of being involved in a project, such as getting social recognition at prestigious events, going to VIP parties, and working with a lot of high energy people. You might additionally encourage the person to talk about him or herself outside of the business setting. For instance, if he or she has photos from a vacation on the wall, you might comment on them and ask how he or she enjoyed the trip.

Should the German Shepherd also have the qualities of a Golden Retriever, then emphasize how he or she will be able to help and support others with your proposed products or services. Emphasize how you or others involved in the project will be trustworthy, dependable, and eager to cooperate, so besides achieving great results from a highly productive team, he or she can expect great teamwork. You can also point out how you or other team members can help to keep things organized and orderly, so he or she will have the benefit of leading a team that works well together, or explain that you will help to help to create such a well-oiled team. Should the German Shepherd type express any concern about budgets, emphasize how the funds will be subject to good controls, so everything will function well. In short, combine your emphasis on getting good results and winning with an emphasis on how this outcome can be achieved in a well-structured, organized way.

Finally, should the German Shepherd appear to have the qualities of the Border Collie, which means having a concern with details, accuracy, and the facts, provide that information to back-up your initial appeal which emphasizes the results and winning. At first, emphasize the results-oriented, success appeal which the German Shepherd type likes, but point up the admiration he or she will get in making this choice. Then, have the facts ready to show why your proposed offering will have the expected results. You don't want to get bogged down in details initially, as you would in appealing to the Border Collie type. But point out that the details are available for later review, and you will be glad to provide them in whatever form the person wants, whether in a file, link to a website, or print-out. Perhaps cite a few supporting facts to show that you know what you are talking about and you have the needed facts to make your case. Then, leave the rest to follow-up, so you keep the focus on how your proposed offering will help the German Shepherd type achieve success and win.

Relating to the Pomeranian (Yellow/Influencer/Fun Party Animal Type)

Suppose you are dealing with a Pomeranian Type. This is someone who is very social. He or she loves to collaborate, work with others, and loves attention and appreciation. He or she is also very high energy, happy-go-lucky, very outgoing, and likes fun, fun, fun.

So come in on that wave length. Take some time to get to know the Pomeranian and engage in some small talk. Show that you have common interests, know some of the same people, go to some of the same places. This way, you start off by developing some rapport and then turn to the business of making your presentation.

A good way to think of the difference in your approach is that dealing with the German Shepherd is like dealing with someone from New York, who is fast-paced and eager to do what you want quickly to get winning results. This approach might be summed up in the words: "Show me the money!!!"

By contrast, dealing with a Pomeranian is like dealing with someone from the Deep South, where you want to relax, like you are at a social gathering with mint juleps. There the emphasis is on having a great relationship that eventually leads to business. But you don't want to push the shift to business too fast. This approach might be summed up in the words: "Show me the love!"

So in relating to the Pomeranian, be friendly, share a joke or two if appropriate, and listen attentively with a big smile, since the Pomeranian loves to talk. Even if you don't feel very outgoing, such as if you are a Border Collie type, try to match the Pomeranian's high energy, enthusiastic style. So smile and gesture a lot, be warm, and show that you hope to work with the Pomeranian like a collaborator on a seemingly fun project that all involved will enjoy.

Taking into Consideration the Pomeranian's Secondary Type

Once you have this fun, friendly, high-energy rapport going, you can take into consideration the Pomeranian's other traits.

If a person is a super Pomeranian type, who is very fun-loving and social, these other qualities may not be very important, In some situations, the Pomeranian may mainly want to have fun and party, which might be more common if he or she comes from a family with money, so hard work is less necessary to get whatever he or she wants.

But otherwise, these secondary choices may be important considerations, if another trait is a close second to the person's primary choice. Here's how to adapt your approach for each one.

If the Pomeranian also has the qualities of the German Shepherd, after you have developed a close connection, you can do your business or sales pitch. When you do such as pitch, focus on the benefits and results of whatever you are pitching. Now that you have warmed up the other person with your social moves, you can quickly pitch the advantages of your project or working with you. For instance, highlight how whatever you do together will be very successful, and that he or she can be in control and gain recognition, no matter how active he or she is in day to day operations. Moreover – and here's where you can bring up the Pomeranian benefits, the person will be greatly praised, recognized, and admired by others who are involved in the project, or who benefit from the work you do.

What if the Pomeranian has the qualities of a Golden Retriever? Then, after all the socializing and schmoozing, talk about how what you are proposing will help and support others. Invite the person to ask questions, since he or she is a good listener, and be calm, cool, and collected, as you present the benefits of getting involved. Talk about the sincerity and trustworthiness of those involved in the program and describe how well organized and coordinated everything is. In short, make this feel like a very comfortable, solid project, since the Golden Retriever likes things to be orderly and stable. Additionally, point out how this project will provide an opportunity to share, socialize, and support others through what you are offering. You might also talk about the opportunities for good fellowship with others, and how you will be there to help attain this vision.

Finally, if the Pomeranian is also drawn to the qualities of the Border Collie, this is the time, after creating a warm fun environment, to talk about the facts or give the Pomeranian a take-away flyer, pamphlet, or workbook with the details. Or perhaps send the Pomeranian a PDF after your meeting with this information. Your goal now is to back up the fun things you have talked about with some solid facts, so the Border Collie can feel comfortable. In other words, the Pomeranian will commonly make decisions and agreements based on his or her gut-level or intuitive feelings, but use the facts and details to justify and support this choice. In this way, he or she can combine fun and sociality with a sense of order, stability, and safety – a perfect blending of Pomeranian and Border Collie, so combine both in your presentation, but start with the appeal to the social and fun-loving Pomeranian and follow-up with the pitch to the fact-loving serious Border Collie,

Relating to the Golden Retriever (Green/Steady/Cool Supporter)

What if you are relating to a Golden Retriever Type, who is very friendly, sociable, cooperative, and supportive? He or she also tends to be informal, and likes order, stability, and keeping things organized.

So in dealing with that person, be casual and sociable yourself. Take some time to be social and show how you like working with others. Point out how what you are doing is designed to help others and that it is a well-organized program.

However, while you want to be friendly, sociable and take some time to develop rapport, the Golden Retriever's style is different from the sociability of the high energy Pomeranian, who likes excitement and is very expressive. The Golden Retriever type likes things to be calm and steady, so be cool and collected as you present any business opportunity or talk about yourself.

For comparison, if you think of the German Shepherd as the hard-driving New Yorker and the Pomeranian as the Deep South party animal, consider the Golden Retriever like the friendly Midwesterner, who likes things to be well-ordered and stable.

Taking into Consideration the Golden Retriever's Secondary Type

Once you've built up rapport by being warm, friendly, and informal, you can consider the secondary qualities of the Golden Retriever. If he or she is a double Golden Retriever, continue to be calm, cool, and collected in your approach and emphasize how helpful whatever you are offering will be.

But if the person also has the qualities of the German Shepherd, shift from being sociable to point up the results and benefits, and how this will be a big win. Don't go into too much detail, though you can provide that later. Now focus on the big picture and state the advantages quickly.

Should the Golden Retriever also have the qualities of the Pomeranian, up your energy and enthusiasm. Talk about how much fun being involved in this project will be. You might point out the social recognition the person will receive from being involved and highlight any opportunities for social gatherings, parties, or other fun things the Pomeranian type loves.

Finally, if the Golden Retriever's secondary type is a Border Collie, add in some facts and details, even a few stats, to support what you have just described. Don't go into as much detail as you would with a full-fledged Border Collie Type, but describe enough to provide that extra supportive detail to show everything has been well thought out and organized.

Relating to the Border Collie (Blue/Conscientious/the Serious Fact Checker)

You'll often encounter fewer Border Collie types at social gatherings or in business presentations, since they tend to be more serious and reserved. They often end up in professions where their concern with details, accuracy, and facts is a real plus, such as being accountants, bookkeepers, computer programmers, scientists, and researchers. Often they are introverts who like being by themselves and working independently, so you may not run into them as much.

But if you do meet them, recognize their concern with facts and details, and quickly point up the evidence for why whatever you are pitching works and provides value. Emphasize its quality, highlight the competence and knowledge of those involved that have contributed to creating a great program. Don't try to spend time with small talk or socializing as you would with a Pomeranian or Golden Retriever. Instead, get to the point. In a phrase, the Boston Collie's approach would be "Just the facts," like a good cop or investigator might say, so honor that. As such, they might be like the old no-nonsense down-to-earth New Englander.

So aside from presenting any facts, highlight your expertise and that of anyone involved in the project. If you or others have degrees or other credentials, mention those. If the person asks probing questions, be prepared to answer them. And if appropriate, have more details available to provide later, or if convenient, give the prospect the supporting materials now.

Whereas other types might feel overwhelmed, Border Collies types tend to appreciate your care and concern for the facts.

Taking into Consideration the Border Collie's Secondary Type

Should the Border Collie's secondary type turn out to be another Border Collie, you've got a Super Fact-Checker, so emphasize the facts and details. Get on your own geek to better relate to the Border Collie.

But if the Border Collie's secondary type is the German Shepherd, after presenting some key facts and details, emphasize the results and the likelihood of success, though point up how the facts support this potential. Also, recognize that while the German Shepherd type may make quick decisions and responds on a gut-level intuitive basis, the Border Collie may want some time to think about things and assess the pros and cons. So provide that space along with the supporting detail, which the Border Collie can review.

Should the Border Collie's secondary type be a Pomeranian, this is probably the most difficult and unlikely combination, since the Border Collie is so interested in facts and details, while the Pomeranian is high energy and interested in socializing and fun. In this situation, perhaps after making the case based on the facts, you might point out how what you are offering might provide a change of pace. It'll be a way to do something different; it'll offer a new experience and a chance to meet some different types of people; and it'll be fun. In this way, you might appeal to the Border Collie's curiosity and desire for new knowledge, combined with the opportunity to develop some good relationships and enjoy collaborating with others.

Finally, if the Border Collie's secondary type is a Golden Retriever, that can be a good combination, since the Golden Retriever is normally calm, cool, and collected, which works well for someone who is interested in facts, accuracy, quality, and details. The Golden Retriever's interest in order, stability, and being ready to adapt and adjust, are also well-suited to the Border Collies' emphasis on accuracy, details, and facts. So if that's the Border Collie's secondary type, after you present the facts, highlight how your offering will help and support others, and explain that it is a well-organized program, which can be trusted to produce the desired results.

Summing Up

In sum, knowing about the different dog types can help you better communicate with and relate to others in a wide variety of situations – from sales and managing people to working with others and finding new clients or a new job.

Initially, note the person's dominant type when you first meet or begin working together. Then, factor in the person's secondary type and modify or build on the first type accordingly.

The chart on the following page summarizes the major way these types might work together and includes a short term that briefly characterizes the 16 types that emerge from combining the primary and secondary types.

The following chapter provides examples of how to best deal with the different types in different situations.

WORKING WITH DIFFERENT DOG TYPES

SECONDARY DOG TYPE	PRIMARY DOG TYPE			
	German Shepherd	Pomeranian	Golden Retriever	Border Collie
German Shepherd	German Shepherd German Shepherd THE WIN-WIN LEADER	Pomeranian German Shepherd THE WIN-DRIVEN PARTY ANIMAL	Golden Retriever German Shepherd THE WIN-DRIVEN SUPPORTER	Border Collie German Shepherd THE WIN-DRIVEN FACT-FINDER
Pomeranian	German Shepherd Pomeranian THE FUN-DRIVEN LEADER	Pomeranian Pomeranian THE FUN-FUN PARTY ANIMAL	Golden Retriever Pomeranian THE FUN-DRIVEN SUPPORTER	Border Collie Pomeranian THE FUN-DRIVEN FACT-FINDER
Golden Retriever	German Shepherd Golden Retriever THE SUPPORT SEEKING LEADER	Pomeranian Golden Retriever THE SUPPORT SEEKING PARTY-ANIMAL	Golden Retriever Golden Retriever THE SUPER SUPPORTER	Border Collie Golden Retriever THE SUPPORT SEEKING FACT-FINDER
Border Collie	German Shepherd Border Collie THE FACT-DRIVEN LEADER	Pomeranian Border Collie THE FACT-DRIVEN PARTY ANIMAL	Golden Retriever THE FACT-DRIVEN SUPPOTER	Border Collie Border Collie THE SUPER FACT-FINDER

CHAPTER 6: USING THE DOG TYPE SYSTEM IN DIFFERENT SITUATIONS

Now that you have a general idea of how the system works, here are a few examples to use it in different situations – to make a sale, to look for a new client at a networking event, to improve your relationships with co-workers, to better manage a team, and to get a job or promotion. Future books in the series will provide more examples from workshops and seminars that are being organized around the country.

The system can help in all of these areas by helping you adapt your message to be more appealing to a particular person, whether you are communicating with a client, customer, co-worker, employee, boss, or other party.

It can help you in your personal life, too, from meeting new people to relating to your partner, family members, relatives, or friends.

Thus, it is a method you can use, along with other information, to make your message more powerful or fitting for the other party. Some other considerations might be the individual's demographics, such as sex, age, education, income, occupation, and ethnicity, along with social and cultural influences.

With this system, you can additionally consider the individual's personality characteristics. If you are already using some of the other personality systems, such as the Myers-Briggs Personality Type, the DISC profiling system, or the red, blue, yellow, and green method, that's fine. Consider the Dog Type system another approach that builds on these other methods, and you can use it to confirm or supplement other personality methods. A key difference of this system is that it uses dog breeds to characterize the different personality types.

Testing Out Whether the System Works for You

A way to test whether the system works for you is to briefly explain the system to some people you already know well enough to type based on what you know about them. Then, tell them how you have typed them and ask what they think of the way you categorized them. Usually they will agree you were accurate in your assessment.

Another way to do the test is to go to an event where you can comfortably meet and get to know people in a relaxed way, unlike the traditional business networking environment, where everyone is trying to impress everyone else with what they can do to help others with their expertise, business services, or products. Then, too, in some business settings, such as a business support or mastermind group, you can feel free to share. Social events can be another place to try out the system, or even if you meet someone in a public place, such at a bus stop or store, you can try to assess what the person's combination of traits might e.

That's the testing method I used while attending a networking gatherings for about two dozen women who were part of a speakers' training program. Unlike the typical networking event, the program leader handed out questionnaires with five business and five personal questions, including "What did you want to be when you were growing up and are you doing that now?" "What do you like to do most in your free time?" "Where would you like to retire?" and "What do you expect that people will get out of working with you?"

To provide some incentive to fill out the questionnaire, the program leader asked us to obtain answers from at least 6 people on two business and personal questions. Then, we should write their name in the blank beside each question and turn in one or more completed slips to enter a drawing for a prize of gift certificate for lunch for whoever's completed questionnaire was drawn.

But no matter who won, the small prize was merely an incentive to get everyone talking and learning about each other. During the exercise, as I talked to different people, I imagined what type of dog they might be. Then, I briefly explained the system and shared my impressions, which turned out to be right.

For instance, I told the high-energy bubbly program leader that I thought of her as a Pomeranian, and immediately she responded: "I love Pomeranians, and I really identify with them." I told a woman who led spiritual enlightenment sessions to empower women that I thought of her as a Golden Retriever. Immediately she smiled and ran her fingers through her long floppy hair. "Yes, that really fits me," she exclaimed.

Next I told a financial adviser and planner, who led wine and empowerment workshops for women and wore a white stylish pant suit that she reminded me of a German Shepherd. And she, too, agreed with my assessment, responding that the Dog Type system seemed to be a lighthearted way to motivate women to seek to increase their bottom line.

Finally, I tried out the system on a woman who asked me four questions and wrote down my answer as I responded to each question. "You just need to write down my name," I told her. But she said, "I like to write down your answer, too, because that helps me remember."

I pegged her as a Border Collie, and she immediately agreed. "I like to keep records of everything," she explained, and when she told me what she did for work, that further confirmed my assessment of her type. She was a social media consultant, but unlike many consultants who were hands on in meeting with clients and advising them personally, she represented a system, and she offered to give me a tour of all the methods for $10. So she was definitely a fact-oriented detailed person, both in her approach to participating in the exercise and in her chosen line of work.

Following are ways you might use the Dog Type system in different situations.

Making a Sale of a Product or Service

You have to do some basic preparation to approach any prospective customer or client to make a sale. When you make your presentation, use the personality dimension to adapt your pitch to be more convincing. Generally, make this pitch when you follow-up after a networking meeting or initial sales call to set up a meeting, though you can do an initial pitch on the phone if you have some information about what someone does in advance.

If you don't have any advance information about the person, perhaps you can get some clue from the type of company they own or are working for. Or use what you know about that company's culture. For example, if you are making a pitch to provide products or services to Uber or Amazon, you know those are very bottom-line companies. In fact, Uber has a bad boy reputation of being very cut-throat or competition-oriented, so make your pitch as if you are dealing with a German Shepherd personality. So get straight to the point and stress the potential for profits and great success.

On the other hand, if you are making a pitch to the owner or rep of a nightclub, hip new coffee house, or event production company, you might treat the person you deal with like a Pomeranian. So highlight how your product or service will add to the fun everyone is having. Of course, you can mention profits, point out how your company is reliable, and add in some facts on your past successes. But keep your presentation upbeat, high-energy, and fun.

Or suppose you are speaking with someone from a service organization, non-profit, or health club. You might start off like you were making a pitch to a Golden Retriever type, because these organizations emphasize support and service for clients. So initially communicate with that vibe, before you bring up profits and facts, or come on too high-energy and upbeat.

Then, if you are meeting with someone in the tech field, that's when to begin as if you are dealing with a Border Collie type, who tends to be conscientious, detail-oriented, and concerned with accuracy and facts. So you might start off by pointing out some of the records your product or service has gained, the number of users it has, how much it has grown because people like it so much, and the like.

An Example of Adapting a Presentation to Make a Sale

To illustrate the process of adapting a sales presentation, based on personality typing, here's how a sales meeting might go.

Jerry has pulled his sales materials and brochures together, and when he goes into the office of the product manager, Sam, he's ready to get to the point. He knows this is a big company in the furniture manufacturing field, and he wants to offer a deal on some supplies they use in the manufacturing process. So he's all set to get straight to the point and emphasize the bottom line of the high quality product he is selling.

Then the product manager bounds across the room toward him, shakes his hand effusively, and leads him to his desk with a big smile. On his desk, Jerry notices some pictures of his wife and kid, and he sees a picture of Sam captaining a boat in a race. So immediately, Jerry alters his initial pitch. Sam reminds him of a happy Pomeranian who loves to leap up, show off, and get petted affectionately by others. So Jerry starts by commenting on Sam's family photos and boating picture. Soon Sam is happily talking about his family and racing for a few minutes, before inviting Jerry to tell him about the supplies he is selling. Thus, the rapport established, Jerry can comfortably talk about supplies, and Sam is eager to do business with him, because Sam likes Jerry, since Jerry appreciates where he is at and responds accordingly. So Jerry makes the sale.

By contrast, had Jerry come in like Sam was a German Shepherd type, he would have come across as too pushy and abrasive, and Sam would have been put off from the get go. So it would be harder to talk to Sam and sell something to him.

Looking for Clients or Referrals at a Networking Event

At a networking event, a primary goal is to meet many people, exchange business cards with them, and follow-up later. Of course, talk to people you already know and share the latest news. But generally focus on getting new business and quickly determining who might be a promising lead or referral partner.

A common approach in meeting people is the 15-30 second elevator speech, where you quickly point up how you can help others with whatever you do, and you ask the other person to tell you about his or her business.

A good approach is to start by asking the other person what he or she does, so you not only find out that information but learn more about the other person's personality type. To gain these insights, look at not only what the person says, but how he or she says it. For example, if the person is very direct, concise, and confident, that's a sign of the German Shepherd. If he or she is very high-energy, upbeat, and sociable, that suggests the Pomeranian. If he or she is more casual and laid back, that might be a Golden Retriever. Finally, if he or she seems quiet and provides a detailed description of a product, service, or company, that's a sign of a Border Collie.

You might also combine an awareness of what the person says and how with signifiers from the person's appearance. For instance, a conservative suit with a power tie for a man and a stylish suit and subdued jewelry for a woman are signs of a German Shepherd. But if you see anything flashy, such as a color tie for a man, or shiny and flashy jewelry for a woman, those suggest the Pomeranian. If the person is dressed more informally or casually, that suggests the Golden Retriever, and if the person's dress is even more informal, out of style, or geeky, that could point to the Border Collie.

Generally, expect to meet fewer Border Collie types at events, since they tend to be more retiring and work behind the scenes. By contrast, German Shepherd types are especially skilled at presenting themselves quickly and well, and Pomeranians and Golden Retrievers like these social events, since they love being around people and they like the enthusiasm or appreciation of others.

What if the other person asks you about yourself first? Perhaps start with the standard elevator speech where you highlight the benefits of what you do, since these networking events favor the German Shepherd's style of quickly getting to the point about the benefits you provide and what you do. But when the other person shares, you can notice the different Dog Type signs and use those for your follow-up, when you call or send an email to set up a further meeting. Then, at the meeting, you can adapt your style accordingly, depending on whether you are primarily dealing with a German Shepherd, Pomeranian, Golden Retriever, or Border Collie.

An Example of Successfully Meeting a Prospect at a Networking Event

To illustrate how to adapt your approach on meeting prospective clients at a networking event, here's how such an event might go.

Sarah is eager to let people know about her health club and its special offer for new members. To pitch this, she has gotten together a pile of business cards, glossy postcards with pictures of the club, and flyers announcing the club's ribbon cutting, tours, and discounts for a day. Thus, armed with her sales literature, she is bubbling over with enthusiasm when she meets and greets new people.

She is especially attentive to name tags which indicate the name of each person's business, and she looks for people who are well-dressed in conservative or stylish dress. They look more like the kind of people who might go to the club, which caters to a more upscale audience in a largely upper-middle class and upper class suburb. As she meets new people, she holds back on her bubbly personality, so she doesn't come on too strong. Instead, she seeks to match her personality with that of the person she is speaking to.

Sometimes to gain these insights, she listens in on some conversations, so she can be ready to approach selected individuals after the conversation breaks up. Alternatively, if the group members have an open stance, suggesting that others are invited to join in, she introduces herself to the whole group.

This approach of sensing who others are before she says anything is a good way to learn about the personality type of the individuals before approaching them, either individually or as a representative for the whole group. For example, if everyone seems very results oriented and all business, she comes on with her German Shepherd persona. If the people in the group are laughing and kidding around as they talk, she puts on her Pomeranian. Should they be calmly having a conversation and seem very comfortable with each other, she becomes her Golden Retriever. And in those rare cases, where people seem to be shy or talking about high-tech details, she similarly tamps down her approach, so she is more quiet and reserved. However, she commonly passes up making a pitch to such a group, since she views them as unlikely candidates for a health club that offers fun social programs.

Additionally, besides listening in before her approach, Sarah looks around for individuals who seem like good candidates, based on their appearance and what they are wearing, since those are cues to personality, too. Alternatively, Sarah might make a comment to someone waiting in the food-line or helping themselves to a plate of food to see how they respond. Do they talk about the food or the venue? Do they mention if they have previously been to one of these business gatherings? Do they comment on how they drove to the event or complain about the parking or the weather? Do they notice what she is wearing and comment on that? Do they immediately smile and ask her what she does?

Their comments are all cues to what their personality might be, since they suggest what is most important to them, and Sarah ticks off the likely associations. For instance, ask what she does right away, and she thinks German Shepherd. Comment on the weather or parking, and that could be a Border Collie. Notice her shiny jewelry, and that might be a Pomeranian. Or if they talk about attending before and how much they like getting to know people from different industries, maybe they're a Golden Retriever.

Then, as she talks further with people she meets at these gatherings, she keeps these principles in mind, adapting her approach as she learns more about the other person. She likewise considers these qualities when she follows up by calling or emailing the people she has met who seem like good candidates for the club or potential referral partners who know others who might like to participate in the club's exercises and programs. Then, she sets up another meeting with people who want to talk more.

Improving Your Relationships with Co-Workers, Your Boss, or Your Employees in the Workplace

At work, the Dog Type system can be a way to have better relationship with your co-workers, boss, or employees. The reason the Dog Type approach works so well in the workplace is that you can have a better sense about how to communicate or interact with someone. The result can be better teams, better decisions about giving assignments to people with different skills and sensibilities, and a better ability to resolve conflicts.

Several personality systems already have a long history of being used in the workplace, such as the Myers-Briggs and DISC approaches, which use a self-administered questionnaire and ratings chart to indicate how well you score for different personality types. Since the Dog Type system draws on these earlier systems to suggest the personal qualities that make up each type, using Dog Types instead of labels or colors works, too. As previously noted, the association of certain dogs with certain personality characteristics is what's new about this system, along with new exercises and techniques that make the process of personality typing even faster and easier and a lot more fun!

Thus, you can readily use the system on your own in thinking about those you work with and how to best relate to them. Or a Dog Type program can be used within a department, division, or the whole company to promote better understanding of the different personalities associated with the different Dog Types. Then, you could use this understanding to promote better communication, interaction, and assignments of roles and activities, based on what a person does best and most likes to do.

Examples of Using the Dog Type System in the Workplace

To illustrate how the Dog Type system can be used in the workplace, here are some examples.

Say your co-worker or boss is like a German Shepherd. You can be more direct and to the point in what you say, and they will be particularly interested in anything that makes the work more productive. Your co-worker may want to know this about the boss, because it can help him do things more efficiently and effectively, which will help to impress the boss. And your boss may be especially impressed, since that will mean the organization, team, division, or department will be more productive, resulting in more profits. In fact, should you have a new idea for a product or survey, point out how this will improve the company's profits. Such ideas may even get you a promotion, bonus, or other kinds of recognition in many workplaces.

Or suppose a boss has an employee who is like a German Shepherd. This might be a good person to put in charge of a team or given more responsibility. If the boss wants the person to do something, he or she should explain this task more succinctly and directly, while emphasizing that this change will make the operations go more smoothly, resulting in more productivity and profits for the company – and perhaps more bonuses and incentives for employees.

What if your co-worker or boss is more like a Pomeranian? When you talk, do so with lots of energy and enthusiasm, and if the co-worker or boss wants, take some time to socialize together. For instance, if the co-worker suggests getting together after work for some beers or wine, go at least once or twice to establish a social, friendly relationship. Then, that rapport will carry over to when you work together, and you may find you have more fun at work, too. If your boss invites the employees to a barbecue or organizes an office party, go yourself and plan to socialize with others you work with, even if being outgoing is not necessary your preferred personality style. You can always leave after an hour or so. The important thing is that you appear for a time to show you are part of the team and can have fun with other employees, which helps to create a more enjoyable workplace, which is what the Pomeranian type likes.

Should you be a boss and you feel an employee is like a Pomeranian, you might take that into consideration in giving out work assignments. Say a Pomeranian has started out working on routine office tasks, such as filing forms in actual file cabinets or on the computer. Maybe the Pomeranian would be more suited to being a receptionist, answering phones, or moving into sales. Or if you are giving the Pomeranian instructions on what to do, perhaps preface your comments with some getting to know you conversation, such as asking what the Pomeranian likes most about the job, or what he or she most enjoys doing, You might even mention what you enjoy doing with your family on weekends, which might help the Pomeranian feel more comfortable and share a little about his or her life outside of the office. You don't want to spend more than a minute or two on such small talk, since you want to maintain the boss-employee relationship, not act like you are creating a buddy-buddy friendship or coming on to an employee of the opposite sex. But a little sociable chatter will help to make the Pomeranian feel more comfortable and at home on the job, since Pomeranians love to be friendly and sociable.

Now let's say your co-worker or boss is more like a Golden Retriever. That means they like helping and supporting others; they hope everyone will work well together and get along. In this case, it helps to show you are a good team player, too. Indicate that you want to cooperate with the group and go along with whatever the group decides. If you give suggestions, emphasize how your idea will contribute to employee morale and satisfaction. Sure it might benefit productivity, profits, and the bottom line, too. But stress how any changes will be a win-win for everyone. Or perhaps suggest activities to help others, like organizing a birthday party for a colleague or getting contributions for a gift for an employee who has had a family emergency.

Or say you are a boss and an employee acts like a Golden Retriever. In that case, you might praise the employee for the ways he or she contributes to the morale and satisfaction of other employees. Perhaps invite the employee to help you or a team leader in organizing an office party, or invite the employee to be part of a welcome committee to orient new employees. Keep in mind that the Golden Retriever employee may not necessarily be the best leader, since that's a role the German Shepherd like to play. But the Golden Retriever likes to help out and support whoever is leading some activity. He or she makes a great right hand or supporting player on the team.

What if a co-worker or boss is more like a Border Collie? Then, you want to share facts and details with them. For example, if you are working with a Border Collie on a project, you might focus on doing the work with little conversation, since Border Collies like doing something carefully and accurately, and they prefer not to have any distractions. Or if you have a conversation about something, you might point out how trends in your industry are affecting your company.

You are less likely to have a Border Collie boss, except in the tech field or academia, since Border Collie types tend to like working independently in the background rather than taking on a leadership role. But if you do have such a boss, be ready to talk facts and stats to them, if you meet with them about something, such as if you have observed a problem in the office.

If you're a boss with a Border Collie type employee, try to find things that the employee has done right to praise, because Border Collies like to be recognized for their skills and abilities, and they like to be known for doing things well. Also, where appropriate, let the employee do things independently or in their own way, so they get the best results, since Border Collie types are often loners, so they do well working on their own. You might also invite the Border Collies to do reports on how a work group is doing, or review any reports that others have done for accuracy, since Border Collies are good at this detailed, analytical work.

An Example of Improving your Relationship in the Workplace.

To illustrate using the Dog Types to improve your relationship in the workplace, here's how it might go for someone working with a Border Collie.

Tony has been tasked by the department head to put together a team to conduct some interviews to see how consumers might respond to a new product the company is considering launching. The goal is to do some in-home and phone interviews, conduct some focus groups about the ad campaign for the product, and try an online survey of Pinterest users. So Tony, selected because he's a good leader and organizer – a combination of a German Shepherd and Golden Retriever, can choose anyone in the company to be part of the team. Most naturally he looks to the individuals working in the sales department or in customer service to do the interviews and focus groups – a good choice, since the individuals in these departments tend to be German Shepherds, who are outgoing, and Pomeranians or Golden Retrievers, who enjoy working with people.

But Tony finds little enthusiasm from the team members for putting the results together. He can barely get the Pomeranians to get their forms filled out properly, and he has to warn the German Shepherds to spend more time getting fuller, more detailed responses from the people they interview. The German Shepherds want to complete as many questionnaires as they can as quickly as possible. So they think if they spend less time with people, they can quickly get useful answers and don't need to probe more deeply. On the other hand, the Golden Retrievers do especially well in spending more time with each interviewee and getting more in-depth responses, which suggest directions for further questions and even new products.

But what to do about the final reports and presentations? Tony finally turns to the market research and accounting departments and finds the perfect combination of qualities in the Border Collies who tend to work in these departments. They are especially good at reviewing all of the questionnaires and tape transcripts from the interviews and focus groups, as well as the results of the online surveys. Then, they are good at synthesizing all of this material into tables and charts showing the main findings about what prospective customers like and don't like. They are also good at preparing the PowerPoint presentations Tony plans to use to present the results to the company owner and investors, so they can decide what to produce and finance for their new line.

Finally, once the project is completed, as a German Shepherd, Tony enjoys the adulation of the boss and investors for putting together the team and coming up with such excellent results, thanks to the hard work of the Border Collie researchers, who put the reports together to show off the work of the team.

Getting a Job or Promotion

If you are looking for a job or promotion, using the Dog Type system can help you, too. In this case, you want to consider the type of the person hiring or promoting you or leading the committee making these decisions.

If you have been working with a boss, you generally already know what he or she is like when you are up for a promotion or seeking a reassignment. So you can adapt your approach for more or different responsibility accordingly. But commonly, you won't know much, if anything, about the new boss doing the hiring. In this case, consider the type of company and what you can find out about the company culture, since besides your skills and abilities, the boss or hiring committee will be looking at who might fit in.

For example, if you are seeking a job in law or finance, the leadership will typically be German Shepherd types. If you are interested in sales or sales management, you are likely to meet a mix of German Shepherds and Pomeranians. Should you be looking at non-profit organizations, government agencies, or health clubs, you are likely to encounter a lot of Golden Retriever types. And if you are approaching a company involved in high-tech, research, or planning, you are likely to find a lot of Border Collies, who are very detail and fact-oriented.

Adapt your job pitch accordingly, though if you aren't sure, imagine that you are doing your pitch to a German Shepherd, where you briefly highlight the benefits you bring to the job and why you are qualified to provide these benefits. Point out how you are very fast and productive in whatever you do, and if you have testimonials or references, mention them, as well.

Suppose you feel the boss or hiring committee are Pomeranian types. Then, show more enthusiasm and energy in pitching yourself and your credentials. Briefly start off with some comments to build rapport, such as talking about how much you appreciate what the company is doing and how you can easily fit in with the group.

If you feel you are pitching what you do to Golden Retriever types, be calm, cool, and collected as you speak about what you bring to the table. Emphasize how you can be a good team player and support others in the company. If the organization is supporting any causes or charities, describe how you appreciate its contribution and hope that you can contribute, too.

Finally, if you meet with a Border Collie type, though this is less likely, since Border Collies tend to work more behind the scenes as noted, support what you say about yourself with facts and details. Offer to show any reports of work you have done. If you have a list of references or testimonials about yourself, hand them over. In this way, you not only show supporting evidence about what you have done, but you show you are a person who likes facts and details, too.

Improving Your Relationships with Others in Your Personal Life

The Dog Type system can also help you in your everyday relationships. Here are a few examples. You may think of many others.

Say you want to give a gift to a family member's birthday. If the person is a German Shepherd type and participates in a sport or fitness regime, perhaps you might give him or her a gift to improve performance, such a device for recording successes. If that person is more of a Pomeranian type, you might give a gift certificate to a restaurant or amusement park, so he or she can take a friend or group of friends to dinner or a day at the park. Should the person be more of Golden Retriever type who is involved with a local charity, perhaps give a gift basket with food and wine he or she can share with others in the group. Finally, if the person is more of a Border Collie type, you might give the person a book with the history of the sport or fitness method.

Or suppose you are creating a team of volunteers to put on an event for a local community group, such as to run a booth a local arts festival or raise money for a charity. You might assign the German Shepherd types to organize and lead a group to do certain tasks, like run the booth or plan to contact local businesses about being sponsors to raise money for the organization. You might assign the Pomeranians types to be the greeters at the both and pour beer and wine. You might assign the Golden Retriever types to answer questions at the booth or go to see the different booths to see if anyone needs help with anything, and if so, get that help for them. You might assign the Border Collie types to write up the schedules and keep track of who is doing what at what times.

You can use this approach to come up with how to best resolve a conflict with a mate or family member, too. If the person is more of a German Shepherd, quickly come up with a solution about what you propose doing or ask them to do offer their solution. Then, if you mutually selection a proposed solution, that's the result. This is the more <u>confrontative</u> approach in the popular Thomas-Kilmann guide to resolving a conflict. If the person is more of a Pomeranian, suggest delaying a resolution of the conflict in order to do something you both like to do in the hopes the conflict will go away or become less important and so easier to resolve later. This is the <u>delaying</u> approach to conflict resolution. If the person is more of a Golden Retriever type, you might spend more time listening to that person's point of view, take into consideration how he or she feels, share your point of view, and suggest a resolution that incorporates what you each want. This is the <u>accommodative</u> approach to conflict resolution. Finally, if the other person is more of a Border Collie type, you might suggest more of a compromise or collaborative approach to conflict resolution, where you each list what you most want. Then, you suggest a compromise solution or you take more time to discuss these different possibilities and come up with a resolution together, which is the more collaborative approach.

Now you can think of other situations in which you can deal with other situations in your personal life in different ways, depending on the personalities of the people involved. Of course, take into consideration what you prefer and feel most comfortable doing; then adapt your preferred style based on the other person's personality type.

CHAPTER 7: QUICKLY IDENTIFYING THE DIFFERENT DOG TYPES

A good way to quickly identify the types of individuals who are likely to be the different personality types is with the DOG TYPE OCCUPATIONS, THINKING, AND EMOTIONAL ORIENTATIONS CHART. You can also use this chart as a quick guide to imagining what a person will be like before you meet, if you are contacting him or her as a potential client, customer, or employer.

DOG TYPE OCCUPATIONS, THINKING, AND EMOTIONAL | ORIENTATIONS CHART

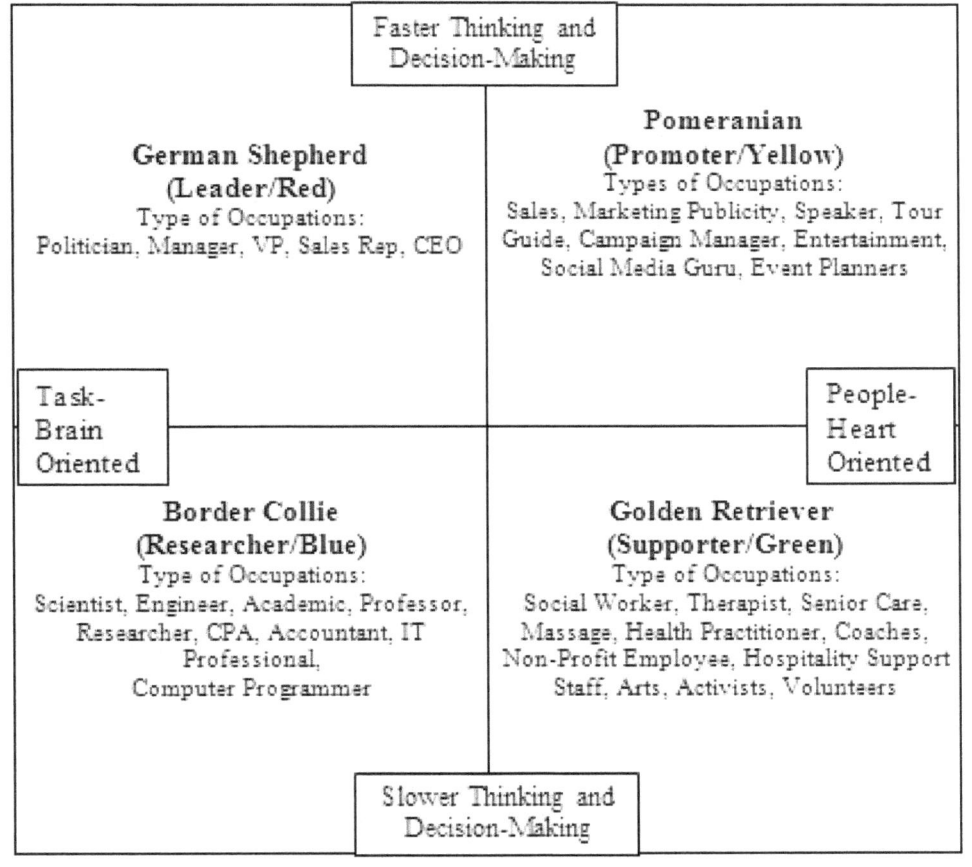

When you meet, you will get other information so you can modify your initial guestimate. Different people will have differing degrees of strength in their most dominant and next dominant traits, and some people may not to fit the usual personality profile for a particular occupation. But in general, this chart reflects a quick and easy summary of what others are apt to be like. You can put yourself on the chart, too, by numbering the categories according to your first (Top Dog), second (Watch Dog), third, and fourth (Underdog) type. In fact, in some systems, your third ranked trait is referred to as your "secret weapon," or here your Sleuth Dog, because under certain situations you can draw on it as an additional strength.

An example might be if you are a real estate agent engaged in an especially difficult negotiation, where your Top Dog is a German Shepherd and your Watch Dog is a Border Collie, while the prospective buyer is primarily a Golden Retriever and secondarily a Pomeranian. You sense that the buyer really wants the house, but is nervous about spending so much money. As a German Shepherd, you are pressing on aggressively to conclude the negotiations and finalize the deal, while your Watch Dog has provided the prospect with plenty of data to show it is a good deal, since property values are likely to go up in the area, due to a booming population, new industries, and a limited supply of homes.

Yet, the buyer is still hesitant. This is where your Sleuth Dog, your Golden Retriever, is what you need to reassure the buyer so you can close the sale. Thus, instead of talking about financial benefits, you should calmly talk to the buyer about how much he or she will enjoy the house and about the support your company will provide to take care of the massive paperwork involved in the sale. You might also remind the buyer about the great schools for the kids, the playground in the nearby park, trails for walking the dog, and the community get-togethers organized by neighbors who want a safe secure community. That kind of reassurance is what the buyer needs to hear so he will feel a sense of belonging to know that this is the right house for him.

The DOG TYPE OCCUPATIONS, THINKING, AND EMOTIONAL ORIENTATIONS CHART also helps to illustrate how the different Dog Types might work well together, if you are looking for partners or employees. For example, a German Shepherd may make a great leader who can sometimes be too hard-driving. But teaming up with a Golden Retriever can provide some balance by offering the warmth and support a prospective client needs to enter into an agreement. Or a Pomeranian might find the perfect employee in a Border Collie, since the Pomeranian is a great promoter who can persuade people to participate in a training program. But he or she may not do well with the details and follow-up, so important tasks may fall through the cracks, such as filling out the necessary paperwork to secure the location for the event or carefully tracking who has paid or not, resulting in some lost income. But with a Border Collie taking care of these tasks, they can be carefully and accurately done.

You can think of other combos and how they can work well together. Some common occupations for each Dog Type are listed on the chart, along with some common characteristics, such as whether a person is more task or people oriented, a faster or slower thinker, and more guided by their heart or emotions or by their brain and reasons.

Using the Dog Type Occupations, Thinking, and Emotional Orientations Chart

To use this chart, record your ratings for each of your Dog Types and create a Circle of Strength in the center to indicate your relative strength in each area. (Or use a Star of Strength with four points, where the positioning of the star reflects the rating – or position the star in the center and vary the point length, so that the longer the point, the higher the rating). Then add the ranking -- #1 for the Dog Type with the highest rating, #2 for the next highest rating, and so on.

For example, if you previously rated your strength in each of the four areas on a scale of 1-10, as indicated on the following page, enter those numbers in the chart for each category. If you didn't previously rate yourself in each area or did so over a month ago, rate yourself now. Then, put that number in the quadrant for that Dog Type. After that, draw and place a circle or star to reflect your relative strength in each area. If there is a tie, break it by assigning one of the pairs a higher or lower number.

To illustrate, suppose you have a rating as follows:
        German Shepherd (Top Dog or #1) – 9
        Border Collie (Watch Dog or #2) – 8
        Pomeranian (Sleuth Dog or #3) - 4
        Golden Retriever (Underdog or #4) – 3

Your Circle of Strength or your Star of Strength would look something like this as indicated on the charts on the following page.

Circle of Strength

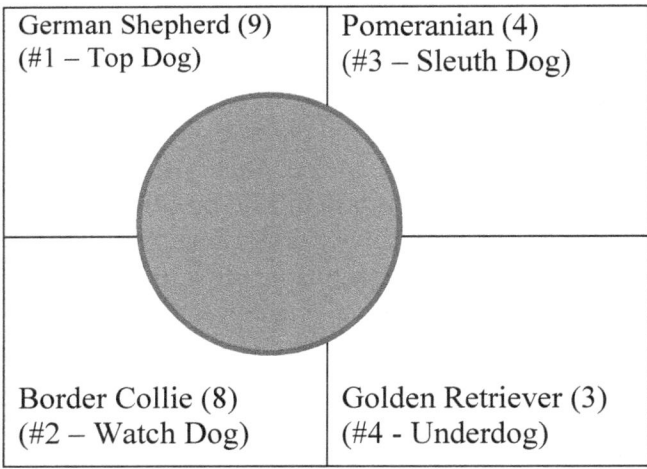

Star of Strength

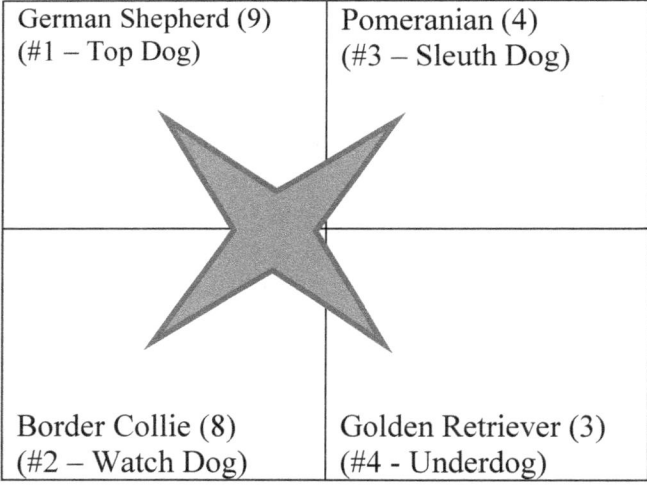

Besides creating a rating chart for yourself, you can estimate where someone else might fall in these four quadrants to give you a snapshot to use in deciding how to relate to that person. Print out the Circle of Strength or Star of Strength chart on the following page to do so. Then, position the circle or star or draw the points of the star to reflect your perception of the relative strength of each of those personality types in that person.

Circle or Star of Strength

Draw in your own circle or star to reflect the relative strength of each Dog Type, and add in the ratings and rankings.

German Shepherd ( )	Pomeranian ( )
Border Collie ( )	Golden Retriever ( )

CHAPTER 8: PUTTING IT ALL TOGETHER

Summing Up

To sum up, the previous chapters have shown how the Dog Type system works and how it can work for you. Much of the focus has been on applying the system in business or the workplace. Additionally, you can apply this approach in your personal life, such as in better understanding your partner, family members, relatives, or friends, and using this understanding to better communicate and interact together.

As discussed, the four Dog Types – the German Shepherd, Pomeranian, Golden Retriever, and Border Collie – build on other personality systems that have been popular both in the business world and in the self-help field. Most notably, these are the Myers-Briggs, DISC, and Red-Yellow-Blue-Green profiling systems. In developing this new system, the dogs selected are very popular dogs that represent each of the four main personality types, though other dogs can be used, if they are more popular in other groups, cultures, or countries.

For instance, some substitutes might be Rottweilers for German Shepherds, Chihuahuas for Pomeranians, Yellow Labs for Golden Retrievers, and Siberian Huskies for Border Collies, since these alternate choices have many of the same personality traits. But preferably, use this system with the selected dogs, since these have already been set up and tested in a series of workshops, and they work. You will also benefit from all the supporting material that has been created based on these four types of dogs.

The chapters in Part II illustrate how to apply these different dog types to recognize your strengths and weaknesses, and how to consider your secondary traits. As described, your primary Dog Type might be viewed as your Top Dog, while your secondary type might be considered your Watch Dog. By combining these two types, you have 16 different types based on an interplay between the two characteristics. As discussed, the system is much like having a superior and inferior personality type in the Myers-Briggs system or being a combination of styles and colors in the DISC and red-yellow-blue-and green color profiling systems.

Then, Chapters 5 and 6 have described how to use your understanding of these types to adapt your approach in different situations. Chapter 5 has discussed what to look for in relating to these different types, while Chapter 6 has provided some examples for adapting your approach to fit the circumstances in four key business situations – making a sale, making connections at a networking event, working with others as a co-worker, boss, or employee, and applying for and getting a job. It also suggests what to do in three types of social situations -- buying a gift, organizing a team for a community event, and resolving a conflict with a friend or family member.

So now you have the tools you need to apply the system yourself.

What's Next?

Going forward, we like to hear from you about your experiences in applying the system, and we'd love to cite your stories in future books.

We are also hope to organize some workshops and seminars using these Dog Types as either virtual or in-person events. These programs will include getting people into groups of different types, so participants can see how they are similar to those in their group and different from others. They will incorporate roleplays so you can try out different approaches with people who have the personality traits of different types of dogs.

Additionally, we are developing a variety of materials to help you in working with the system, including workbooks, training videos, online courses, and fun things you can use to get the conversation going and connect with others. For instance, you might imagine yourself wearing a T-shirt that says: "What's your Dog Type?" or "I'm a German Shepherd and Border Collie…What Are You?" with pictures of these two dogs. Then, too, there might be dog mugs with dog faces, calendars featuring the four dogs and subtypes, and postcards with the images and qualities of different kinds of dogs. There might even be a game in which you can become different dog types and race to achieve a goal.

In short, we have all kinds of ideas for building this Dog Types system.

At the same time, for the millions of people who love cats, we hope to create a parallel system based on cat types. In this system, people can select the type they most identify with from four types of cats, such as a Savannah or Bengal Cat, which is tough like a German Shepherd, or Ragdoll Cat that is fun and friendly like the Pomeranian. This way, as you prefer you can use your Dog Type profile, Cat Type profile, or both. The systems and methods will be exactly the same, except that one will feature dogs and the other will use cats.

So now that you know the system and how to apply it, start using it to have more success in your business and at work, as well as better relationships in your personal life. And let us know the results. As a German Shepherd and Border Collies myself, I'd really like to know.

ABOUT THE AUTHOR

GINI GRAHAM SCOTT, Ph.D., J.D., is a nationally known writer, consultant, speaker, and seminar leader, specializing in business and work relationships, professional and personal development, social trends, science, and crime. She has published over 50 books with major publishers. She has worked with dozens of clients on books and proposals on popular business, self-help, and memoirs. Additionally, she writes film scripts and has produced 10 feature films, documentaries, and TV series. She writes the copy and works with a team of associates who help clients with social media posts, publicity, promotional videos, and web design.

She is the founder of Changemakers Publishing, featuring books on business, psychology, self-help, and social trends. The company has published over 200 print and e-books and over 150 audiobooks. She has licensed several dozen books for foreign sales, including the UK, Russia, Korea, Spain, and Japan.

She has received national media exposure for her books, including appearances on *Good Morning America, Oprah,* and *CNN.*

<u>Her books on business include:</u>
Work With Me (Davies-Black Publishing)
A Survival Guide for Working with Humans (AMACOM)
Lies and Liars: How and Why Sociopaths Lie (Skyhorse Publishing)
<u>Her books on self-help, health, and wellness include:</u>
What's Your Dog Type? (Changemakers Publishing)
Discovering Your Dog Type? (Changemakers Publishing)
Mind Power: Picture Your Way to Success (Simon & Schuster)
The Empowered Mind: (Simon & Schuster)
Want It, See It, Get It: Visualize Your Way to Success (AMACOM)

Her films in distribution include *Driver* (Gravitas Ventures), Infidelity (Green Apple), *The New Age of Aging* (Factory Films) and *Me, My Dog and I* and *Rescue Me* (Random Media). The films are showcased at www.changemakersproductionsfilms.com.

Scott is active in a number of community and business groups, including the Lafayette, Pleasant Hill, and Walnut Creek Chambers of Commerce. She does workshops and seminars on the topics of her books and on self-publishing.

She received her PhD in Sociology from the University of California, Berkeley, her JD from the University of San Francisco Law School, and five MAs at Cal State University, East Bay, including in Anthropology, Mass Communications and Organizational/Consumer/Audience Behavior, Popular Culture and Lifestyles, and Communication.

OTHER BOOKS BY THE AUTHOR

What's Your Dog Type?

Discovering Your Dog Type

Mind Power: Picture Your Way to Success

The Empowered Mind: How to Harness the Creative Force Within You

More Success and Happiness

Affirming Your Success

Turn Your Dreams into Reality

The Vision Board Book

100 Ways to Gain More Success

CHANGEMAKERS PUBLISHING
3527 Mt. Diablo Blvd., #273
Lafayette, CA 94549
www.changemakerspublishing.com
(925) 385-0608 . changemakers@pacbell.net

www.ingramcontent.com/pod-product-compliance
Lightning Source LLC
Chambersburg PA
CBHW081754100526
44592CB00015B/2427